BECOMING MANDELA

To Jane

BECOMING MANDELA

Be Your Legacy

TREVOR WALDOCK

FOREWORD BY PETER HAWKINS

Epub ISBN: 978-1-7399651-1-2

Book ISBN: 978-1-7399651-2-9

Cover by Andy Stewart, www.unbelievablebook.uk

Contents

Foreword

Discovering Eldership

In early 1999 I was travelling from Johannesburg to Cape Town by plane and was privileged to find myself sitting next to Alfred Baphethuxolo Nzo, who was Foreign Minister in Nelson Mandela's first Cabinet, from when Mandela was first elected President in 1994. We talked of the recent history of South Africa and the changes that were coming about. He told me how he would stand down as a Minister and a politician at the forthcoming election. But soon Mr Nzo turned the conversation to families. He proudly showed me pictures of his children and grandchildren.

I said, 'Well, once you are retired you will have more time to spend with your grandchildren.'

He looked at me sternly and said, 'Life is different in our culture; we do not retire. Once you step down as a leader, you become an Elder. An Elder has their own responsibilities. One of which is to hold the Leadership to account. The leaders have to answer to the Elders for what they do, and we must support and nurture them.'

Immediately I felt a sadness and a lack within my own life and that of my culture. The personal lack I had explored many times in psychotherapy, in workshops with Robert Bly, and with my spiritual teachers. I had searched out and been blessed to have some great mentors. But the cultural lack of Eldership in our politics, professions and communities was a new awareness that I would pursue. So when I met first met Trevor Waldock in 2003, I discovered a shared quest and was enriched by the conversations we had prior to his writing his book *To Plant a Walnut Tree*. I was honoured that Trevor included a number of the stories from our conversation in that book.

Since that time, I have been a great admirer of the way that Trevor has continued to pursue this quest in a very committed and active way, developing leadership programmes for young leaders in communities across Africa. He develops leadership in others, not by knowing better, but by constantly discovering through collaborative inquiry with the young people what is needed in their communities, and what needs affirming in them, so they can step up and respond.

Just recently I watched a video from Trevor's work, of a young black female community leader in Africa saying: 'Please stop talking about us as tomorrow's leader's, our societies cannot wait that long. In Africa, we are today's leaders.'

As I write this, I have just been watching the speeches of the young people's gathering in Spain, prior to the COP26 Climate Conference that will be held in Glasgow in October 2021. Impressive young leaders from around the world, who are desperately trying to hold the politicians of the world to account for the lack of turning their rhetoric into committed action and for the horrific legacy they, and we, are leaving for their generation to contend with. I despaired as I then listened to the patronising empty rhetoric of the older politicians' responses. Where, I thought, are we Elders who have a role to play, not in adding more words, but in helping the powerful leaders really listen, emotionally feel and take on board what the young leaders are telling them? We need to help the political leaders have the humility to ask young people for their help. Where are the Elders who are needed to facilitate a true generative dialogue between the generations and between the rich, early industrialised nations that have caused the bulk of the greenhouse gases, directly or indirectly, and the economically poorer countries who disproportionally will suffer the consequences. There are some, but far too few.

Sadly, Mr Nzo died later in the year I met him, so was not able to fulfil the Eldership role he spoke of. However, as Trevor demonstrates, Nelson Mandela did live long enough to show us how it is possible to move from Leadership to Eldership. You become an Elder when you give up on personal ambition and attachment to specific outcomes, but can do what is necessary to be done, without seeking reward or recognition. When you can respond to life's challenges non-reactively, drawing on wisdom, not knowledge or expertise. I have written about Eldership in a number of my books and other writings, but still struggle daily to give up leadership and respond as an Elder.

My best teachers have been my grandchildren. There is a lovely Welsh saying: 'Pure love arrives with the first grandchild.' This is because the deep love you had for your own children comes around again, but this time you are not so psychologically entangled. You can love your grandchildren for who they are and are becoming, without expectations, or the same anxieties, fears and replication of your previous family patterns.

As I write this the first Autumn leaves are being blown by the wind and rain past my window and I am grateful that several weeks ago we managed to get the hay into our barns just in time. I'm also grateful for the many fruits and vegetables from our garden that are sitting in the covered area outside our kitchen. I remember the harvest festivals I have attended over the years, when we sang with thanks for what we had received from the rich earth and nature around us. I am reminded of a recent conversation with colleagues with whom I am editing a book on how coaching can make its contribution to the climate emergency and how we discussed the importance of practices of gratitude. I found myself saying to them: 'But we must not stop at gratitude, appreciating the enormous amount we receive by grace from the wider ecology every moment of every day. At harvest festivals (which could be celebrated daily) in all the different religions and indigenous ceremonies that I know of, after we have given thanks, we move into offering.' As Robin Wall Kimmerer writes in her beautiful and wise book *Braiding Sweetgrass*: 'Cultures of gratitude must also be cultures of reciprocity.'[1] And she beautifully describes First Nation Americans' ceremonies where everyone puts into the collective collection what they do not need and takes out what is necessary for them.

When I was young, I thought privilege was something you strived for and earned and that it bought you freedom. Only now in my seventies can I look back and realise I was always, and will always, be privileged and that the more privilege you have, the more it brings you not freedom, but responsibility. I now believe this is what Mr Nzo was trying to teach me. To still be alive with our health, our faculties and a family is to be greatly privileged. With that privilege comes greater responsibility.

Thank you, Trevor, for being a role model and sharing your wisdom and inquiries and active experiments into how we become responsible Elders and Ancestors.

Peter Hawkins, Barrow Castle, Bath, UK

October 2021

Introduction – letters to my sons and daughters

When I was nineteen years old, I spent my summer working in a medieval castle in Upper Austria, as part of the staff team focused on international youth work. One changeover day, I'd been working hard swapping a hundred duvet covers on beds in numerous dormitories. The windows of the adjacent rooms were all wide open and the sweet, warm air of the mountains was wafting its way from room to room. But then I was summoned to a meeting, and I walked anxiously towards the common room at the end of a long corridor. 'Had I done something wrong?' was my immediate thought.

When I entered the room, I was greeted by the two friendly faces of George and Connie, my supervisors in that pivotal summer of my life.

'Thanks for coming by,' they began. 'We've been watching you work over the past few weeks and we wanted to tell you how much we appreciate you. Not just what you are doing, but how hard you are working and your attitude to it all and your care for the guests.'

I found myself breathing out in relief when I felt the incoming tide of affirming warmth. I had been seen.

One afternoon a few weeks later, I was invited to tea with the director of this international youth centre. Over a Stollen cake and with George by my side, the director was also very affirming of me, what I was doing and how I was doing it. He cut to the chase by asking me back the following summer to work with all of the European youth programmes.

'Of course, you'll need to learn German to do the job,' he added.

I'd tried and failed to learn French at school, so this could have stopped me in my tracks. Yet his belief in me encouraged me that I could do it – and I did.

Those words, those affirmations, that invitation truly became a game changer for my life. No one had ever really seen my potential before and called it out. My father's attitude to me felt like it oscillated between indifference, irritation and anger. So when kind words were addressed to me, it was like water to a parched soul in the desert, like an explosion of life deep within. What if those same words had been spoken to me by a gang leader, a drug runner, a paedophile? The story would have been very different. I've stockpiled many stories of young people whose whole life direction was determined by an adult's word of affirmation – 'you can do this' – or of discouragement – 'you'll never be an artist, engineer, writer, leader...'.

Years later, when I learned about the neuroscience of the brain,[2] it all made sense. A young person's brain is hardwired to want to live a meaningful life, to make a difference in their world. Yet when there is no adult calling out an invitation to them, they can easily take their unrealised potential to the grave. One word spoken by an elder can make the difference. When the hunger in a young person's life to have their potential seen meets the recognition of someone older, it finds a home in positive hearts and minds, and powerful and meaningful things start to happen.

Zeid Ra'ad Al Hussein, former United Nations Commissioner for Human Rights, expanded on this burst of possibilities:

> Young activists are the drivers of movements for justice, human rights, the environment and an end to discrimination – just as every strong movement for human rights and solidarity in history has been spearheaded by the young.

Think of South Africa[3] and the pivotal role young people played in ending Apartheid; think of Greta Thunberg on the climate crisis; think of Boyan Slat[4] on cleaning up the oceans. Think of the scores of young social entrepreneurs being inspired and fostered through organisations like One Young World[5] and the Yunus Centre.[6] All of these young people and thousands more are responding to the call of the late Dr Babatunde Osotimehin, then Executive Director of the United Nations Population Fund,[7] who challenged us all that we need to put young people at the centre of solutions to global problems, not just leave them to be inheritors of our problems:

> Young people must be at the centre of the ... vision for sustainable development to drive the future we want.

Those of us who are middle-aged were young people not so long ago. We set out on a life journey to make our mark in the world. How are we doing with those dreams? Maybe we feel we've achieved them, maybe not, but the need to have a life mission doesn't go away. As Jay Blades, author of *Making It*,[8] said, 'When you don't have a direction/purpose you will end up everywhere and nowhere.'[9] Holocaust survivor Viktor Frankl wrote (paraphrasing Nietzsche), 'Those who have a "why" to live, can bear with almost any "how".'[10] That core 'why', or meaning or purpose, is necessary across the whole life span, as an anchor and a compass to navigate our 'three score years and ten'. But what often happens is that we get disheartened and give up our aspirations, or we lose our way through the busyness of life, or we become 'weary of well doing',[11] or we hold on to a leadership role too long, because we cannot bear to face the loss of identity that we fear awaits us in the last decades of our lives.

The support and help that most of us have lost are the elders in our lives, as well as the aspiration to be an elder ourselves. Traditional societies always knew that beyond the triumphs and failures of the first half of life, beyond the highs and lows of leadership, lay eldership. Those older, wiser people have perspective, experience, courage, insight and empathy. They are people who have made the journey ahead of us – both internally and externally. While we need young leaders to emerge from this rising generation, 'great leaders are formed in the cradle of elders'.[12]

Nelson Mandela was one whose life was shaped by the presence of elders from his birth until his death. He often spoke of their importance in his becoming. We all need elders in our lives to shape who we're becoming. Nelson Mandela wasn't born the person we came to respect – he grew into that man through a journey of becoming.

Ask yourself: 'Who am I becoming? Who do I want to become?' As a business leader said in anguish the other day, 'The world is on fire... and what am I doing about it?' And young people may well ask us, 'Yeah, what *are* you doing about becoming an elder for us to look up to?' For the many of us in the second half of our life or approaching it, the question is what *we* are doing to make a difference, to leave a legacy.

Steve Jobs was successful in the first half of his life and ended up being fired by his own company, but when he returned to Apple he became a different person – a person who created a top organisation that has outlived him. Jim Collins (author of *Good to Great*, *Built to Last* etc.) has researched this dynamic[13] and demonstrates that almost every name we associate with greatness and success was not that person from the start. They *became* that person. Dwight Eisenhower, Eleanor Roosevelt, psychologist Edith Eger, Wendy Kopp (Teach For America), Gordon Moore and Robert Noyce (Intel), Bill Gates (Microsoft), Ed Catmull (Pixar), Phil Knight (Nike) – all *became* the people they are now known for being. The title of Michelle Obama's autobiography sums it up – *Becoming*.[14]

They were all willing to take the long road to mastery and eldership, not the quick route to short-term success. This is why it's urgent that we help young people start the long journey to becoming elders in their own lifetime. You can't fast track, or microwave, true maturity.

But we need to start with ourselves. If we're not becoming elders, then how can we offer the invitation to the emerging generation to do so?

The call to be an elder is the difference between success and mastery. Everything around us – TV culture, our peers, Facebook – is calling us to be successful, whether through our looks, our profile, our income, our status. Success is not wrong, but it is short-lived. In contrast, eldership is a lifetime journey that takes the long view of your life – the legacy view. As one of my mentors once said to me, 'The most useful thing you can do with your life is to plant a walnut tree... because you probably won't see the fruit in your own lifetime.'[15] The fundamental question we should find our way towards is: 'Who do I live for and what am I going to leave behind that is going to benefit others?' History shows us that the really 'successful' people play the longer game. Success is a one-week wonder, whereas eldership is a lifetime investment.

Most of us in the West didn't grow up with many role models of elders, or if we did we didn't call them by that name. The concept of eldership may feel quite strange and alien. We had glimpses of such people, but while being inspired by them, we simultaneously dismissed them as somehow special: 'Oh, yes, I see them as elders... but I'm not like them.' We quickly write ourselves out of the possibilities of our own potential. We write ourselves out of the legacy script.

Yet as James Hillman defines it, *extraordinary* people are simply examples of what the *ordinary* person can become. They give us an invitation, not a red card. I can never be Mandela, nor should I try to, but I can become my own version of him. All the qualities we admire in him he learned over a lifetime, and I can learn each of those qualities over my lifetime too.

As I write this, I'm the same age Mandela was when he was still in prison, serving a life sentence on Robben Island, yet he faced each day as a student and invested in who he was becoming. *Any of us can start the journey of becoming today, regardless of age or circumstance.*

I have written this book as a series of imaginary letters, conversations with my sons, my stepdaughter, my daughters-in-law, and the many young people I mentor around the world. I use the word 'guys' in the neutral sense, to cover both genders. I invite you to listen in and join me on this journey with them, so that you can begin your own journey of becoming your own unique version of Mandela that the world calls you to be. At the end of each chapter are three questions that you can answer for yourself, but ideally you will sit down with your peers, or even someone younger, and discuss them together. The chapters are designed to start a conversation, but if you really want to invest in learning more about the subjects covered for your own life, then The Youth Compass Project (www.youthcompassproject.com) can provide you with a free, online, in-depth learning journey.

I offer this book as an invitation to you to embark on your own journey of becoming - to help you invest in what it means for you to leave a legacy.

CALLED BY LIFE

1. Mandela & me

Hi guys

I don't think I ever told you about my visit to Robben Island.

It was in the heat of late November 2014 that I climbed aboard the ferry *Susan Kruger* and journeyed across Table Bay from Cape Town. I was on my way to that iconic island, a place that had seen the tragic incarceration of over 1,500 long-term prisoners during the Apartheid years. Eerily, the *Susan Kruger* was also the same boat that took Nelson Mandela and so many other prisoners across the 4.3 miles to Robben Island back in 1963 – six years after I was born. The boat had been doing this run since 1959 and was looking like it might not make too many more crossings!

I felt connected to history from the moment I got on board. Ahead, to the east, was Robben Island, but behind, to the west, for the whole trip was a breathtaking view of Table Mountain. It is such a poignant crossing. For two hours you're trapped in feeling like you're either in the belly of Jonah's whale or in HG Wells's time machine. Beneath my feet was the rusty hold in whose darkness countless prisoners had been chained, and you can't help but meditate on the excruciating reality of injustice, of what people can do to their fellow humans. You find yourself looking forwards and backwards at the same time, not just to Table Mountain and then to the island, but from the present to the past and back again, between the cosmopolitan vibrancy of Cape Town and this raw window into South Africa's painful history. The crossing suspends you in a weighty transition between the present and the past.

That memorable crossing gave me the chance to reflect on my own life journey and what had brought me to this place at this time. As you know, Jane and I lived and worked in South Africa for the last three months of 2014 and half of 2015. While Mandela was everywhere in spirit, this was our first connection with the man himself. We were on a journey to connect the dots of history, mine and Mandela's, if that doesn't sound too grandiose. Mandela had been in the back of my mind when I started writing the book *To Plant a Walnut Tree*.[16] He was an example of what the book was really about – what lies beyond leadership as we get older. Around the time the book was being published, Mandela, along with Richard Branson and Peter Gabriel, formed what they called The Elders,[17] a group of independent but very experienced, wise statespeople, who could speak neutrally about the world's most pressing challenges. When I was researching the book, I tried, through my South African friend Nicki who knew people from his community, to get an interview with Mandela, but he was very old and his health was failing, so he wasn't taking visitors. I'm glad I tried, though. If you do nothing, if you don't try, then *nothing* is what will definitely happen.

In my youth I'd had only a background consciousness of the man and a sense of the global engagement with his struggle. I remember sitting late one night in Ronnie Scott's jazz club in London, listening to a South African artist singing that Apartheid rallying cry of a song, 'Bring back Nelson Mandela', calling for his release from prison. I developed an increasing interest in him as a leader and an elder in the following two decades and my range of Mandela experiences grew, specifically over the months that followed that trip on the *Susan Kruger*. And you will recall when we all made that emotional visit to the Apartheid Museum in Johannesburg years later; such a harrowing experience.

I remember the trip I made to find Mandela's birthplace in Qunu, on the Eastern Cape. It was a challenging hunt for his house, getting a speeding ticket, spending hours in the car, but I eventually found it, although you can't get very close to the actual house. What the long drive did was give me time to digest the poverty and isolation that surrounded his childhood years. Of course, he did have the advantage of his family background, which many of his young friends didn't.

On another occasion I stood at the gates of Victor Verster prison near Paarl, in the Western Cape (now named Drakenstein Correctional Centre), and tried to imagine the crowds at the moment when he walked free, punching the air with his fist. A statue stands there now to remind everyone of that day and that triumphant moment.

One time we went north to Orange Farm, the township that sits adjacent to Soweto, where the young Mandela grew his confident wings as a lawyer and activist. I still feel burdened by the hopelessness I saw engulfing the young people in that sprawling world of shanty shacks.

The great surprise was the time we booked into a wonderful small guesthouse on the shoreline of Paternoster, on the Western Cape, with its unending miles of unspoilt beaches. On arriving we discovered that Mandela and Graça Machel had actually stayed at that very guesthouse, after he retired as President. We sat on the sofa he had sat on. We stood in the bedroom and touched the bed he had slept on.

The guesthouse host told us of the couple's daily routines, Machel's gentle chiding of Mandela when he was being stubborn, and his morning ritual of reading a pile of newspapers from across the world that were delivered to him, even though he was no longer 'working'. That private routine, even after he had retired, told me that he was a man of the whole world and someone who was still hungry to learn. Perhaps the most moving story we were told was about the day he visited a local beach restaurant in Paternoster. When it was discovered who the guest was, the news spread like crazy. Within the hour, hundreds of children were crowding for a view of the great man. Rather than brush them away, he sent his trusted aide, Zelda la Grange, to buy up as many sweets as she could find and then line all the children up when he had finished his lunch. Mandela took the time to shake every child's hand and give them a sweet. That defines the man for me.

When the *Susan Kruger* finally docked at Robben Island, I could feel, like everyone else, that every moment of the next two hours would be a walk in the footsteps of unforgettable history. We were shepherded on the tour of the island by a man who had himself been a political prisoner there during the Apartheid years. He knew the history first hand. He showed us the quarry where prisoners had mindlessly broken rocks and where the sun's glare, reflecting off the white stone, had damaged Mandela's sight for life. Our guide spoke with the gravitas of a man who had slept in those appalling dormitories, with their hard floors, glassless windows open to the elements day and night, and had experienced the humiliation of everything from beatings to inadequate clothes to pathetic food rations.

The epicentre of this experience for me was walking towards the cells that had housed Mandela and his friends who were in there for life – the solitary confinement wing. We held back and let everyone in our group go ahead of us to look into this cold, hard space. We wanted to be the last to arrive at his cell. We didn't want to be rushed. When we arrived at the pale blue bars of the cell, everyone else was chasing the guide to the garden of the exercise courtyard, where Mandela had hidden his drafts of *Long Walk to Freedom*. In the silence of this private moment, I stepped inside the open cell next to Mandela's locked cell and drank in the atmosphere. In his day the windows had bars and no glass to stop the winter rain beating in. He didn't have a bed, just a bedroll made of a thin blanket. I was shocked by how small the cell was, too. I checked no one was around and then lay on the cold floor. My head was touching one wall and my feet the other. I am 6′ 2″ and Mandela was 6′ 4″. Nothing else needs to be said.

What I never told you was that I went back to Robben Island four months later. Our friend Lennox was a child of Apartheid. He had told us his stories of shame and humiliation and oppression, about being turned away from cafés, told there was no room, when it was clear the café was three-quarters empty. He spoke with pain about his mother's violent arrest, coming home from school and having no idea where she was, and the kindness of neighbours who supported him and his brother through the trauma until she was released. Nelson Mandela, Ahmed Kathrada, Steve Biko, Walter Sisulu, Oliver Tambo, Albert Luthuli, Robert Sobukwe, Denis Goldberg, Helen Suzman, Joe Slovo, Ruth First, Leon Sullivan – there wasn't one name of the heroes of liberation that Lennox didn't know. I asked him one day if he had been to Robben Island and he said he'd never been able to afford it. So Jane and I took him with us for our second visit and this time we saw the whole experience through his eyes. The most unravelling moment for us was standing with him when we reached Mandela's cell. Although the cell was still locked, Lennox collapsed, clinging to the bars, and wept. We watched powerless as his grief for and gratitude to Mandela poured out. He was talking quietly as he wept and we wondered who he was talking to, so we edged a little closer and it was Mandela – he was thanking him, truly from the bottom of his heart.

Some moments in life you don't forget. This was one of them. I hope you meet Lennox one day. We often say that he could walk with kings. Life has shaped him well.

I'm going to stop here. There is more about Mandela that I want to share, but I can explain another time why I think he is important for our relationship and our future. I hope I have given us all enough to embark together on a detective trail.

Much love

Dad

STARTING A CONVERSATION

1. As you reflect on your life so far (young or old), who do you look up to as a role model of growing old well?
2. What are the characteristics and virtues of the older people you most admire?
3. What do you know of their personal history that may have shaped the person they became/are becoming?

2. Missing persons

Hi guys

You both know I've been a lifelong fan of playwright Arthur Miller, ever since I read *The Crucible* at school. Then, at age fifteen, I experienced what it was like to cry while reading a book for the first time, emotionally hijacked by *Death of a Salesman*. Recently I re-watched a performance of *All My Sons*,[18] a heart-breaking story on so many levels. As I write to you, I'm remembering when the dad, Joe Keller, has a sudden realisation that his life decisions didn't have an impact only on his own sons, but on everyone's daughters and sons – hence the title.

I don't have to tell you that I'm getting older; not old, but older. My own father is dead and I hadn't realised until recently just how much I grieved the lack of the mentorship kind of relationship I craved with him. Maybe I was able to ignore the loss at the time because you guys were young when he died and I could throw myself with even greater passion into being 'super-dad'. I wanted to be the dad for you that I never had. But suddenly you've left home and become fathers to your own young children.

I've been left with confusion – both about becoming older and about my worth and my usefulness to those who are younger, like you. Not just *my* sons and daughters, but *all* sons and daughters. Do I, or my generation, have anything to offer all the younger people who are striding out onto the adult stage of their own lives? I'm confused because I was a son who needed not just someone older, but someone elder.

Someone who was a model of wisdom, courage, inspiration and integrity; someone who could call me up to my potential and call me out when my ego was getting in the way. Confused, because I didn't come close to getting what I needed. Confused, because I got a second chance to experience fatherhood when you guys were born. Confused, because I became your hero, playmaker, rainmaker, mentor and champion. Confused, because one day you grew up and I wasn't needed in the same way.

It was in my confusion that I reconnected with the writings of the famous 'older' who became an 'elder', Nelson Mandela. I shared a little of my journey with him in my last letter to you. What does he have to say about this dilemma of the generations? I became interested in discovering what role elders had played in shaping him. And what I discovered amazed me. Who he was and who he became were shaped by the presence of elders across his *whole* life. Elders were central to his *becoming*. We talk of Mandela, but Mandela talks of the place of elders from his childhood right through to his death. It made me want to place a missing persons ad in the newspaper, for all the elders we've lost in our communities. We are missing the necessary ingredient in what made Mandela the man he was. No one seems to have noticed it or talk about it... so I'm going to do just that.

Of his own childhood Mandela said, 'In my youth in the Transkei, I listened to the elders of my tribe telling stories of the old days.'[19] He grew up surrounded by the voices of his elders. You could ask what on earth his elders, with their experience of an unglobalised, rural, localised environment, could offer the young Mandela, who would go on to face the whole world? You could easily imagine him turning to these old guys in the village and arrogantly saying to them, 'What do you know about the real world?' Instead, he looked back and saw their input as foundational to his future success and wisdom.

When he was fifty-seven years old, he said, 'I still respect our elders and like to chat with them about olden times when we had our own government and lived freely.'[20] Even as he entered that phase of life called 'getting older', he was still drawing wisdom from his elders.

Then at eighty years old, speaking to the UN International Year of Older Persons, he said decisively, 'A society that does not value its older people denies its roots and endangers its future.'[21] A tree without roots cannot handle storms. Mandela's view was 'no roots = no future' – and the roots are the relationship the upcoming generation has to its elders.

At ninety years old, how did Mandela sum up his vision for the role of elders in society? He said that 'using their collective experience, their moral courage and their ability to rise above the parochial concerns of nation, race and creed, they can help make our planet a more peaceful, healthy and equitable place to live'.[22]

South African writer Reuel Khoza notes that leaders of the quality of Mandela are formed in the cradle of elders.[23]

We all need elders:

- Their collective experience.
- Their moral courage.
- Their perspective.
- Their wisdom.

All of these are essential ingredients in who we are becoming. But I'm not sure that many people look to their elders for such things any more.

Mandela did, from cradle to grave. The existence and vital role of elders in Mandela's whole life were foundational to who he became.

I had lunch with some friends the other day. Surrounded by oak beams and flagstones from a converted old barn, now a restaurant, we talked about our children becoming adults, about ourselves growing older. That led on to the subject of olders (people whose age keeps on mounting) becoming elders (people who are like the 'roots' Mandela spoke of). I told them what I had discovered about the role of elders in Mandela's life and asked them the obvious question, 'Is there still a place for elders for our young people?'

They said unequivocally, 'Yes, definitely.'

I asked them whether they thought young people had a key role in helping olders to become elders.

Again, their reply was an unequivocal 'Yes'.

So, what should we do? In many ways, conversation between younger and older people is dying out. I see it in my own life and I see it all around me. Do I just let it go? Do I just say 'That was then, this is now; life moves on'? Or do I take courage from Mandela and find a way to restart this conversation between the generations?

That's why I'm writing to you guys – to try to open up this conversation. But I think you knew that already. ☺

Love

Dad

STARTING A CONVERSATION

1. What did you (young or older) learn from specific older people in your life?
2. What would you like to have learned/be learning from those who are older?
3. Do you think there is a role for elders in our generation? Why are there so few of them around these days?

3. Becoming Mandela

Hi guys

It was lovely to see you both together in the same place this weekend – a rare treat. When you were little kids you were inseparable, and then one day you both grew up and went in your own directions, so it was a joy for us all to be able to walk these endless fields together. I'm glad you're up for this conversation. I'd forgotten you had since been to Robben Island; call it a 'senior moment'.

Do you remember when we went to listen to Desmond Tutu speak at the Sheldonian in Oxford? Of the many hilarious and challenging as well as heart-breaking stories he told us about the Apartheid years, one thing stuck with me. It was something he echoed in his book with the Dalai Lama, *The Book of Joy*,[24] where he says:

> When he (Mandela) went to prison, he was a very angry young man. He was commander in chief of the military wing of the ANC. He firmly believed the enemy had to be decimated and he and his comrades had been found guilty in a travesty of justice. This is the guy who went in.

But something happened over those incarcerated years. As Tutu goes on to explain,

> Twenty-seven years later he comes out kind, caring, ready to trust his erstwhile enemy.

The Mandela we came to know and love in his later years, Mandela the elder, wasn't always *that* Mandela. As Tutu points out, he *became* Mandela. The reason that idea caught my attention is that I realised it is true of both me and you. I am becoming someone. I'm not the finished article yet. You are becoming someone too. Who you are now is not who you were when you were eighteen or will be in fifty years' time. It's a fact of life. I remember exactly where I was when the question hit me. I was crossing the bridleway on the bottom field and I found myself thinking about Mandela and in the same moment asking that question of myself: *Who am I becoming?*

It's a sobering thought. Every day I am becoming someone, just as Mandela, every day from his childhood until his death, became who he became. A man who was intentional, a man of larger vision and purpose, an inspirational leader, empathic, courageous, resilient, wise, deep, a man of perspective and of moral authority. He wasn't always those things when he was younger. He became them. Something happened as he went through his life experiences. Within the child and young Mandela were as much the seeds of anger, murder, revenge, aggression, and terrorism as all of those good things I described above. Mandela *became* Mandela through the little things he did every single day, moment by moment, decision by decision, decade after decade. Each moment of his life was a moment of becoming.

I realise that as I'm describing Mandela's journey, you will both be smiling that child-to-father smile. I know you will want to question why on earth I am even putting myself into the same sentence as Mandela. It's true: when people like Mandela reach iconic status, they also seem to become untouchable to us mere mortals. We admire them, but from afar, as unreachable heroes. We love who they are, we want to be like them, but in the same breath we know we never will. They are the exception.

Interestingly, Mandela saw himself as rather average:

> I sometimes believe that through me, Creation intended to give the example of a mediocre man in the proper sense of the term.[25]

And I want to challenge this unreachable hero idea about the man. Something I learned from my readings of the inspirational psychologist James Hillman has also shaped my thinking. He said that rather than view exceptional people as impossible to aspire to, they are, in fact, just a highly visible example of what can be true for *all* of us 'mediocres', the vast majority of the world. As I thought about that, I realised it was true. All of those good characteristics about Mandela that I mentioned a moment ago – wisdom, empathy, courage – all of them can be developed by anyone. They just shone brightly in him, so we could all see what human greatness looks like in action. This is what I mean by *becoming Mandela*. I can be inspired by the characteristics of this spotlighted, very human person. Let me give you two small examples.

I remember when I had my first experience of Brexit rage. We were having dinner with friends and of course Brexit came up, because the leave date was fast approaching. Suddenly, out of what seemed like nowhere, the husband became very confrontational, in a personal way. I decided to back off and we survived the evening, but I felt hurt, wounded, angry. It was hard to sleep that night, but as I chuntered over what had happened, a thought grabbed me in the wee small hours: What would Mandela do in this situation?

It's so easy to read about how he was attacked, oppressed, shamed – not just for twenty-seven humiliating years in prison, but for all those years earlier – and say, 'Wasn't he amazing... wasn't he forgiving... isn't it brilliant that he learned empathy rather than revenge?' But Mandela wasn't naturally empathic, forgiving and conciliatory. He learned to be that way. How did he learn it? He learned it every time he experienced one of those 'dinner party' moments across the decades of his life. He would have had endless sleepless nights of strong emotions and aching for revenge, but he learned to become Mandela by how he dealt with his response to every little incident. This challenged me to grow, to learn, to change, to use this painful event to become someone different than I would naturally be. It wasn't easy. I didn't want to 'give in', but I worked on myself and I did choose some different responses than I would normally have had.

Another example happened recently. As you know, after fifteen years I finally decided to step down from leading Emerging Leaders. As the founder, it was very tough for me to do this. There aren't too many road maps for founder CEOs stepping down, so where could I get help? I went back to Mandela and he taught me two things. First, I had been tempted to a slight despair over what I would do next, because I still have my energy and passion for justice. I feared I was going to be left on life's shelf for however many years still remain. I remembered that Mandela didn't even leave prison to become President, let alone all the other stuff he did, until he was seventy-two years old. That gave me hope and perspective on my own situation. The other thing was that he intentionally only served one term as President, when everyone wanted him to continue. He knew the important leadership step of ending as well as beginning. As Richard Stengel, Mandela's biographer, observed:

> In many ways Mandela's greatest act of leadership was the renunciation of it... he had set the course and now it was time for others to steer the ship.[26]

The study of how he left was a source of courage and wisdom for me in my own leaving.

All that Mandela became, through the choices he made each day over his lifetime, shines the light of possibility on who *I* am becoming, who I could become, who I want to become. All of us can learn all of the qualities we admire most in Mandela. This realisation allowed me to continue to sit with the question of who I am becoming. I had never, up to that point, so clearly and consciously asked myself whether I am becoming who I actually *want* to become, or if I even know who that is.

I played a little mind game with myself recently. I imagined a dream-like scene in which I am invited to a very comfortable theatre in my hometown. I am shown to my seat on the front row and as I walk down the aisle, I see that the room is full of everyone I know: my partner, my children, my siblings, my relatives, my close friends and my distant friends. Also in the audience around me is everyone I have ever met at work, in my community, at the gym or wherever. When we are all settled down, the master of ceremonies (MC) points to someone on the back row and they stand up. Everyone is silent. The air is so full of anticipation you can hear the sound of your own breathing. The MC then asks the standing person this one question: 'Who are you becoming?'

After a short pause the reply comes, 'I'm becoming more corrupt.'

No one seems fazed by the answer – it was expected.

The MC points to the next person and asks the same question, 'Who are you becoming?'

'I'm becoming more trustworthy.'

A few silent nods from around the audience.

Again and again the MC goes through the rows of people. Each one stands and each one gets asked the same question, 'Who are you becoming?' The answers that flow are as diverse as the people in the room:

'I'm becoming more cynical.'
'I'm becoming more hopeful.'
'I'm becoming more empathic.'
'I'm becoming more trivial in my conversations.'
'I'm becoming more inclusive with people who are different than me.'
'I'm becoming more fearful about my old age.'
'I'm becoming more passionate about justice.'
'I'm becoming more patient with my children.'
'I'm becoming someone with greater depth.'
'I'm becoming unreliable.'
'I'm becoming irritating.'
'I'm becoming more courageous.'
'I'm becoming...'

And so the MC continues for a few hours and everyone gives an answer. When anyone in the audience hesitates or falters, unsure what to say about themselves, the friend next to them nudges them and gives them an honest prompt with a loud stage whisper:

'You are becoming more bigoted.'
'You are becoming a better listener.'

'You are becoming a little softer towards those you disagree with.'

'You're becoming more selfish.'

Finally the MC pauses. The auditorium is totally silent, as if everyone is holding their breath. He then points to me and I know the question he is going to ask before the words even leave his mouth: 'And you, Trevor... who are you becoming?'

That's when I wake up from my mind game.

I'm reminded of a true story from my past that I never told you about. I was about twenty-four and your mum and I had just moved to Cambridgeshire to start my new job after college. I was young, raw, insecure and desperately wanting to seem older than my years. Some friends had invited us round for a dinner party and as it turned it out there were only six of us. One of them was Eddie, the real and fictional character in *To Plant a Walnut Tree.*[27] After the meal was cleared and the dishes washed, there was that slightly awkward moment of silence in the conversation, where you know it's too early to make your excuses and leave and yet there really isn't much else to talk about. Eddie must have sensed this and so he suggested we play a game. As if he read the rise in anxiety in the room, he immediately tried to calm our fears by naming the game we could play. He called it 'I want to be like you'. Of course, none of us had heard of it before and we were still nervous, because we had no idea what kind of game it might be. It turns out the game he was proposing was a version of 'Who do you want to be?'

We were all given a small square of paper, about Post-It note size, and a pen and we had to secretly write down who we wanted to be at age eighty. We were being asked to project our current selves into our future selves and put a name to who we thought we might most aspire to become. There were a few minutes of groaning and anxious noises, but when we were ready, we folded up our bits of paper and put them in a hat. One by one, each person drew out a screwed-up piece of paper, unfolded it to reveal to them alone what the name was, and then call it out to everyone. The group had to guess which of us had chosen this particular name and why we thought so. It was a bit of fun and certainly not your average mindless party game, but as I look back, what intrigues me most about this game is that I *knew*. At twenty-four years old, I knew in an instant who I wanted to become at eighty. I didn't need to pause for a moment to work it out. Without hesitation, I wrote down the name Paul Tournier.

I can't remember if I ever mentioned that name to you, or whether you saw his books on my shelves in the study when you were browsing. It really doesn't matter that virtually no one knows who he is, only that I did. I have no idea how I originally came into contact with his writings. I think the first book of his I actually read was *Escape from Loneliness.*[28] I had encountered it as an undergraduate, living in a London suburban bedsit and experiencing real loneliness for the first time in my life. Paul Tournier was a Swiss psychologist who coined the phrase *médecine de la personne* (medicine of the person). Maybe today we would use the term 'holistic medicine'. He was a doctor and a psychiatrist who advocated treating the whole person as a physical, emotional, psychological and spiritual being, rather than just treating part of them. His conviction was that as humans every part of us is interconnected and a problem in one part is a symptom of a problem in the whole. At the time of this dinner party he was an older man, but what was most captivating was that he was truly an elder. That's what I wanted to be.

To be clear, I didn't want to be a doctor or a psychiatrist, but I could clearly see myself at eighty years old sitting in front of a roaring log fire talking with people about their life journey: walking with them in thinking through who they were, what a meaningful and purposeful life would look like for them, and how to create some personal road maps to get there.

As a younger man I had aspired to be Paul Tournier and had clearly seen the 'older', or 'elder', that I wanted to become. Even though I hadn't met the guy, he was helping me imagine something meaningful and purposeful – a bigger self for my future.

As I said earlier, what still strikes me now, decades later, is that I somehow knew at twenty-four who I wanted to become. I would love to ask you both that question someday. We've never really discussed it together. I chatted to my friend Steve the other night about this question and he said that the young people he knows would fall into two categories if you asked them who they wanted to become. One group would relish the challenge of being asked and the other group would hate it. I asked why and he replied: 'Because it's too threatening to be asked a question as personal as that.'

What do you think, guys? I'd be interested in your thoughts. To my mind this question – for both me and you, my friends and your friends – is the first gift Mandela has given us.

I'll write more next week. Until then...

With love

Dad

STARTING A CONVERSATION

1. Talk with each other about who you think you are and who you think you are becoming.
2. If you could change in any clear way (like Mandela went from angry to kind), what one area would you most like to be known for?
3. Who would you name that as an eighty-year-old (roughly) you would like to become and why?

4. Do not linger

Hi guys

I know you love to call me 'old man' and I'm fine with that. I take it affectionately. I remember when I was a kid and I looked ahead to the mythical year 2000, which then seemed a lifetime away. I used to sit and calculate how old I would be that year – forty-three – and I used to think how *old* that was. Now I see that I was barely getting into my stride. I mentioned in a board meeting the other day that I was coming up to sixty-two and the two older men in the room laughed at me as if I was a teenager!

Let me go back to that party game I told you about, the one with Eddie, and how it was that I knew who I wanted to be when I was eighty. What was it in me that had connected the young man I was then with the older man who I had a (probably very idealised) vision of? Building on those Mandela quotes about elders that I shared with you the other weekend, there was a further reflection when he was in prison, thinking about his own relationship as a young man to the older men around him. He said:

> Western civilization has not entirely rubbed off my African background and I have not forgotten the days of my childhood, when we used to gather round community elders to listen to their wealth of wisdom and experience. That was the custom of our forefathers and the traditional school in which we were brought up. I still respect our elders and like to chat with them...[29]

What was it about these older men that he respected? He said they were wise and full of experience. What does it take for a younger person to want to listen to their elders? I've just witnessed Boris Johnson dismiss the likes of Ken Clarke and Lord Soames (Winston Churchill's grandson). Other people in positions of power have dismissed Betty Boothroyd and Baroness Armstrong. Total disrespect and casting aside of the elders.

And how did these older men in Mandela's life actually become elders?

I've been observing a problem in my own generation for years. The way I would frame it, to steal from Mandela again, is that a lot of people linger too long when they get older. Let me explain.

When Mandela came out of prison, he was seventy-two. Up to that point he'd had a purpose, a cause, a mission. His whole life's energy was geared up to fight. They called it 'the Struggle'. It would be an understatement to say that when he came out of prison, he was tired and he deserved a rest. None of us would have denied him that. But this is what he said:

> I have walked that long road to freedom. I have tried not to falter; I have made missteps along the way. But I have discovered the secret that after climbing a great hill, one only finds that there are many more hills to climb. I have taken a moment to rest, to steal a view of the glorious vista that surrounds me, to look back on the distance I have come. But I can rest only for a moment, for with freedom come responsibilities, and I dare not linger, for my long walk is not ended.[30]

'I dare not linger.' I have seen many colleagues around my age winding down, seeking ease and taking the foot off the pedal of aspiration. Just yesterday two different people told me they were retiring. One is younger than me and the other is my age and semi-retiring. I don't have any issue with them stopping doing what they are doing... but for what? Cruises? Coffees at the local garden centre? Are they unwittingly choosing to linger?

In my early twenties I had a friend, Paul, who in his thirties was both a great bass player in a blues band and an exceptional photographer. It was Paul who first introduced me to BB King. I used to enjoy talking to him, because of his dreams and aspirations. For me he embodied talent, creativity and possibility. I found him inspiring. He could have been a professional musician or a professional photographer, or both. But as I continued to meet with him over that decade and into his forties, I slowly realised that he wasn't going to do anything. It was all talk. Fear, apathy, lack of confidence, lack of intentionality – I don't know what stopped him. He got *older*, but he didn't become an *elder*, and I realised I'd lost the desire to hang out with him. The inspiration had gone. He just seemed to have become tired. He'd lingered too long.

I also remember a guy called Mike who I was coaching. He had a high-pressure job in an investment bank in London. When I first met him I knew he was in his early forties, but his grey-faced look made him seem more like mid-fifties. As he talked about his work, I could sense that the life had gone out of him. I dug a little deeper and he told me how, when he was younger, he wanted to go to university and train as an architect. He loved shape and form and construction and he was very good at drawing. When he told his dad he wanted to pursue a career in architecture, his father ridiculed the idea and told him that architecture wasn't a good career, it was too insecure, and that banking was a much safer direction to go in. 'You'll never be without a job in banking' was the advice he got. So he took the banking route and he told me how much he had hated every day since then.

I could go on. Your granddad was the same. As a young engineer he got a good job working at a coal-fired power station in north London. With the birth of the new generation of nuclear power stations he was scooped up, with a group of hopeful, ambitious young men, and trained up for this new era of power. It was like being taken on by Google or Facebook in our day. The future looked full of unlimited possibility. I watched him in his forties, the light slowly dimming in his eyes. I witnessed him taking safe steps and drifting into a weary resignation of running down the clock into his fifties and towards an early retirement of golf and stamp collecting. He got 'older', but he didn't get 'elder'. He lingered too long.

I know these are the unattractive stories and there are many other positive examples, like Mary Robinson, Edith Eger or David Attenborough, but my point right now is that I'm asking myself whether I am becoming the kind of elder Mandela talks about. The kind of wiser, experienced person who becomes an important part of the fabric of younger people's lives. Or am I just getting older? What I find interesting is that from his youth Mandela had elders in his life. He respected them and aspired to be like them... and he did become like them. He became Mandela.

The other day I talked to Jake about this question. I figured he would have a perspective as a newly turned thirty-year-old, and he did. We were taking a long walk across the fields by our house (the ones we walked ourselves recently) and as we strode out, I asked him who he would look up to as an elder for wisdom and advice, or for mentoring in his life. He stopped abruptly, looked at me in clear surprise and said, 'I wouldn't!' I pushed him a little further on his response and he repeated that he wouldn't seek the advice of those who were older:

> Why would I? My generation voted to stay in the EU and you didn't listen to us; my generation are screaming for urgent action on the climate crisis and we see you respond like nothing is happening! Why would I seek the wisdom of people who, to be quite frank, don't seem very wise?

And for the final punch he added, 'To be honest, if I needed advice, I'd go on Google!' His honesty took my breath away, but it was hard to disagree with him.

A couple of years ago I watched Greta Thunberg, the now globally famous young person from Sweden, addressing the United Nations conference over their woeful inaction in not declaring the issue of climate change an emergency and dealing with it as such. Her speech was clear and reasoned. She was demonstrating the rare courage of speaking truth to power, but at the end of her talk there was only polite applause. I was truly shocked. There should have been a thunderous, standing ovation. Thankfully she wasn't diverted from her mission. I was left wondering whether that was a snapshot of our times.

I saw it again when I heard about Boyan Slat from the Netherlands. At the age of twenty-three he created The Ocean Cleanup,[31] an ambitious vision to remove plastic from the oceans. When he conceived the idea, he went to one hundred older business leaders for financial backing. Ninety-nine of them ignored him and the other one told him not to be so stupid and to give up, because it couldn't be done. Thankfully he didn't listen.

What troubles me for your generation when I hear these stories is where are the elders? Where are the Mandelas? Where are the people you can look up to who embrace the energy, vision, passion and commitment of young people and engage with them to add the wisdom, perspective and experience of years? Even as I say this, I know there are excellent role models around. Internationally we have the likes of Paul Polman, Graça Machel, Naomi Klein, Jimmy Carter, Desmond Tutu. People like these are clearly elders, with a public profile. But I guess what I'm also talking about is the everyday people like me and you, when you are older.

I have loved watching you both grow up. Your vision, your innovation, your hunger for life have been a joy to witness. The psychologist in me isn't surprised at all. Adolescence is the period of identity formation, of asking 'Who am I?' in terms of your emotional, intellectual, social, sexual identity. The prefrontal cortex of your young brain, the newer part, is all set to be woken up, engaged with, inspired to purpose, meaning and making a difference in the world. I have been doing some informal research over the past few years. When I have met young people who seem to be inspired to be activists or change makers, I have asked them to tell me the story of how they began. In almost all cases there was an older person, a teacher, an uncle or aunt, a coach or a parent, who inspired them to become who they are becoming. Someone who said to them, 'You can do this; I will stand with you.' Every young person's brain needs an older person, a Mandela, to be a role model, to awaken them to their potential and support them as they make that journey.

Youth development is a serious biological business! As scientist and teacher Joe Pearce says:

> If a child's environment does not furnish the appropriate stimuli needed to activate prefrontal neurons... the prefrontals can't develop as designed. Their cellular growth itself becomes compromised and faulty.[32]

Between the ages of fifteen and twenty-one, the brain is putting on its track shoes, taking off its tracksuit, getting on the running track of life and ready to go somewhere. But where? And how? And what if there aren't good role models to help? Productive young people can quickly become destructive, or self-destructive. I hope I have been able to actively cheer you on and give you the confidence, and at times the wisdom, to chase your uniqueness.

What I'm struggling to say to you both is this. As a young person, like I was once and you are now, we need the help, wisdom and guidance of older people. Mandela had elders around him from a young age and continued to have them all the way through his life, with men like Walter Sisulu as his lifelong mentor. But it's not just young people who need the elders: us olders need the youngers. As an older person I need help to not linger. I need your help to keep me growing into the kind of person a younger person needs. You and I both have the same need. We are both faced with the same question, 'Who are we becoming?' And we are both faced by the same challenge of lingering too long. For my generation, that is lingering too long in the place of the easier life; for you guys, it looks more like lingering in the swathes of distraction that surround you. We need each other to keep leaning into this journey called *life*. We need each other to prevent complacency and sluggishness, or settling for a compromised life.

These questions are age neutral and age embracing. I was feeling their pull at eighteen, at twenty-one, twenty-four, thirty-four. Even if I wasn't consciously asking these questions, neuroscience and experience tell me that the questions were always pushing for answers. I'm still on this journey and you and your friends are still on their journeys and your gorgeous little children are just starting out on their exciting journeys too.

If I'm honest, this is what has driven me to write these letters to you. Even though you are both living in different parts of the world, how can I, how can we, create a conversation with each other, as well as me with myself, that can help us to work out:

- How can we become intentional about life, or become an inspiration to other people?
- How can we develop wisdom and depth, rather than superficiality, as we grow older?
- How can we grow courage or gravitas?
- What would it mean to develop greater perspectives on our ego, our suffering and our mortality?
- How can we become leaders who leave a legacy?
- And finally, can we create conversations to help others with their journeys?

I'll continue to gather my thoughts and will write again, but I'd love to hear your thoughts before I do.

Much love

Dad

STARTING A CONVERSATION

---

1. Do you see examples of people you know who got 'older' but not 'elder'? What do you notice about them and what can you learn from them?
2. Why do you think older people linger too long in their life journey of development? What can you learn from this?
3. Where do you see your own greatest danger in your life journey in lingering too long?

SHAPED BY LIFE

5. Purpose – live in service of something bigger

Hi guys

I know you both like bikes, so you'll appreciate an insight I had yesterday (a flash of the blindingly obvious). I thought that when I got on my bike I was the one in full control, making it move, determining its speed and direction. Actually, that is only part of the truth. The journey the bike makes is shaped by a dynamic combination of gravity working on us and on the bike, plus friction, inertia, wind resistance, gyroscopics, weight, skill and aerodynamics. The same is true of life. My point is that there is what *we* do in life, our actions, but the many other obvious and hidden pressures and forces of life also shape our journey. There is the 'push' from *us on life* and there is the 'push' of *life on us*. How we creatively work with both the *me-push* and the *life-push* constitutes what shapes our life's journey.

I've been thinking a lot about Mandela, as you know. What is clear to me is that his whole life was shaped by *me-push* (like his activism for justice) and *life-push* (life acting on him: poverty; the Apartheid system) and his responses to that *life-push* on him, his further *me-push* (him on life). It was a lifetime dance. At no point did Mandela wake up and say to himself:

> Hmm, I wonder what I can do with my life. What are my strengths? What are my gifts and abilities?

> What are my hopes and ambitions? Ah yes, I think I'll end Apartheid.

It didn't happen that way. Life called him through a set of circumstances that he was uniquely born into. Life had him born in a certain place, at a certain time, and he saw things that he couldn't ignore. Mandela's whole life was driven and shaped by a passionate purpose, which was to end injustice in the shape of Apartheid. His passionate purpose was his response (me-push) to the call of his circumstances (life-push). If Mandela had been born in a different country at a different time, he would have become a different person.

I think we have got it all upside down. We have become so used to self-focused questions like 'What do you want to do with your life?', which I think is maybe the wrong question. Surely, life itself is calling us. Surely life is confronting us with all kinds of needs that it has for reparation, survival, rebuilding, reshaping, sustainability, civility, justice, equality. What is our response? What is the world calling me to do? What does the world need from you?

Last week I heard Nobel Prize winner Muhammad Yunus say to a few thousand young people:

> Look around you. What do you see that's wrong in the world? Start a business to fix it.[33]

This call on our lives doesn't stop at a particular age. Life keeps on calling to us until the day we die. I'm still asking myself these questions each day. That's why I have such a problem with the idea of retirement. It's as if we can say to life, 'I'm sixty-five, I've served my time working, so I'm going to stop listening now and go do my own thing.' We have become so used to trying to call out people's *ambition* that we have lost sight of their *vocation*. Vocation comes from the

Latin word *vocare*, 'to call'. Life, it seems to me, is calling us. Some people would even say that *through* life the Divine is calling us to take action that serves or benefits something beyond ourselves (people and planet).

A few years ago, I spoke at a school in the south-east of England. The way the day had been set up was that in the afternoon I would work with a large group of over a hundred (terrifying) twelve- and thirteen-year-olds to introduce them to the idea of leadership. Then in the evening, I would do a session with their parents.

In the afternoon I remember clearly standing in front of this intimidating group of kids and asking them a question:

> What do you see going on in the world where you find yourself saying, 'This is not OK; I want to do something about this'?

What happened next took my breath away, although I don't know why I was so surprised. They all hunkered down in groups of three or four and started talking very intently. There was no mucking about. They were very focused. When I stopped their discussions and asked who had ideas, every single hand went up. With an expectation of a lot of similar ideas born out of adolescent groupthink, I started going around the auditorium one pupil at a time to find out their big idea. There were as many different answers as there were pupils! They were bursting to share their outrage that the Amazon is on fire; there was horror that polar bears are so threatened and that the ice caps are melting; they were appalled that children their age were being trafficked; they couldn't get over their indignation that people are still living in extreme poverty or that vast numbers still have no access to clean water; and they spoke with concern and compassion for those affected by flooding in their local community.

What I concluded was that all young people see global issues very clearly and that the screaming needs of the world are already calling on them. Take the youth climate protests around the world right now as clear proof. I guess the question is: 'What does it take to help young people to own and validate their own questions, their own call, and to start moving towards doing something about it?' We know Greta Thunberg did it with climate crisis. We know Boyan Slat did it with ocean plastics. But they, as well-known icons of action like Mandela, are just there to remind everyone else that they can also do something, even if hardly anyone gets to hear about it.

Do you remember Harry, who baby-sat for you when you were kids? I remember having a conversation with him one grey afternoon over coffee in Costa. He was debating with himself, using me as a foil, about whether he should start an MBA, or change his job, or do this or do that. Having known him for years I couldn't resist giving him feedback, because I was observing something in him that he seemed to keep replaying. I told him it seemed like he lived his life as a perpetual observer. He was like the guy watching the football game from the stands (bleachers), but never getting on the pitch to actually play. It was as if he was holding back on everything: job moves he wanted to make, relationships he wanted to pursue, ideas he had but wasn't taking action on. I asked him what was stopping him getting out of the spectator stands and on to the pitch and actually playing, rather than always talking about it. He had all this energy, but something was missing. Where was the call? The passionate purpose?

What I am clear about is this: Mandela had a larger purpose for his life that set a blazing fire underneath all of his other attributes. I'm pretty convinced that without this one thing, this passionate purpose, we would have never heard of the man. A passionate purpose was what animated his ideas, his values, his possibilities... his potential. That purpose was what he woke up to and what shaped each day of his life, but it came from a response to unspoken questions: 'Mandela, what does the world need from you? Who are you here to serve? What is your life going to be in service of?'

It seems to me that the important insight here is realising that life is calling out to all of us, not just Mandela. It was true for every one of those children in the class that day. It was true for Harry. It was true for me growing up hearing about the Biafra famine as a ten-year-old and responding by starting up our school's own branch of the Save the Children Fund. Personally, I don't think we are ever too young to be asked such questions. And it seems to me that our brain is demanding it of us. As I told you in an earlier letter, the prefrontal cortex, the newest part of our brain, is designed to be called to when we are young. The brain is crying out for someone to ask it: 'Who or what is your life in service of? What's your bigger "why" for your life?' What is scary is that the brain is deeply wired in young people to be meaningfully called to. Why is that scary? If that doesn't happen, the brain will then pick up other voices calling the person to do something *negatively* meaningful, like joining a gang, running county lines[34] or other destructive behaviours that get people's attention. It's no surprise that so many of our communities seem to be in a destructive spiral. Who is calling their young people to a meaningful life? Where are the elders?

For Mandela that bigger purpose, the one that shaped all of his talents, education and ideas, was his passion for universal justice. He said this at his inauguration in 1994:

> Let there be justice for all. Let there be peace for all. Let there be work, bread, water and salt for all. Let each know that for each the body, the mind and the soul have been freed to fulfill themselves.[35]

In Judaism there is a saying to the effect of 'You don't have to feel responsible for changing everything, but you don't have an excuse to do nothing'. In fact, being overwhelmed by the size of the call that is facing us can be a good thing. It can call out a deep purpose and a big vision.

We make saints out of people like Mandela because they have a very clear and passionate, defining purpose to life and we all get to hear about it. But when he was a kid in Qunu, no one knew Mandela, apart from his friends. No one knew Mandela, apart from his friends, when he was living in Soweto. Mandela had a purpose he was so committed to, he wasn't looking to be famous for it – he was even willing to die for it:

> During my lifetime I have dedicated myself to this struggle of the African people. I have fought against white domination, and I have fought against black domination. I have cherished the ideal of a democratic and free society in which all persons live together in harmony and with equal opportunities. It is an ideal which I hope to live for and to achieve. But if needs be, it is an ideal for which I am prepared to die.[36]

This echoes a tweet from writer and activist Frances Moore Lappe, quoting IF Stone: 'If you expect to see the ultimate result of your work, you simply have not asked a big enough question.'[37] Mandela had such a big question that shaped his life's purpose.

It is my view that we *can* create a passionate purpose for ourselves. I think that Mandela, as an icon, provides a blueprint for the rest of us. What my own experience has taught me, especially that day in the classroom, is that we should start with what is right in front of our noses. Mandela's nose was pushed into the realities of Apartheid, injustice and inequality. These were unavoidable. The problem is that we can actually avoid the unavoidable. We can pretend we don't see what is in front of us, we can walk around it, ignore it, rationalise it, but it's still there. The difference for people who want to develop a passionate purpose in their lives is that when they are exposed to something they let it get the attention of their heart as well as their head.

Take John Bird and Gordon Roddick. Thousands upon thousands of people walk past homeless people living on the streets in our towns and cities every day, but these guys stopped and let what they saw get to them. They faced their discomfort, powerlessness and inexperience and they said, 'This is not OK. We have to do something.' The result? *The Big Issue*,[38] a global outreach magazine that allows homeless people to earn an income with a quality product. The passionate purpose, the big idea, the big why, the one thing – call it what you will – starts with what is in front of us and it may go no further than one simple response, a single action, or it may grow into something bigger. Whether it does or doesn't become something bigger is irrelevant. What matters is having some purpose that is bigger than ourselves. That is what will drive us to grow into bigger people, to realise our true potential.

For Anita Roddick it was environmental sustainability and human rights campaigning for prisoners. For Edward Timpson it was the challenges of fostered children and youth unemployment. For someone else it might be reducing the speed of cars racing through their village for the safety of children and the elderly, or befriending lonely people in the community, or addressing the loss of trees, or rewilding our grass verges. As the classroom of children showed me, the issues are almost infinite and they are all in front of our noses, or eyes, every day. We just have to let one of them get our attention.

I can think of a number of things that have driven me over the years, but as I look back on some of the earlier ones, I feel they were driven more by my ego than by a passionate purpose. If I'm honest, looking like a hero, trying to find significance, ambition, doing something of impact - all of these were big motivators for me. Maybe that's inevitable in the first half of life, but I would have really valued someone older who I trusted, who could have helped me navigate sorting through these issues of my motivation - the ego thing - while pursing the calling, the vocation.

I don't think I ever really told you about the time I was having to choose my academic subjects for the final two years of schooling (A levels). I had been absorbed with cycle racing all over the country in the preceding years and so had done enough at school to be OK, but not much more than OK. Suddenly we were expected to know what we wanted to narrow down and study, because we were meant to know what we wanted to do with our lives! I had no idea what I wanted to do and I had no guidance from anyone older, so I just made some quick choices. Bad choices, as it turned out.

I would have loved an elder who could have journeyed with me through such a key point in my life.

Thinking more recently, starting Emerging Leaders was a good example for me of 'just start, even if you have no idea where this is going, or what you are doing'. I never set out to create a charity at all. I just got on a plane to Zambia in 2005 with a friend. Emerging Leaders as an idea was born out of that trip. It was reinforced by every other desperate place I visited over the next few years: Zambia, Rwanda, Uganda and Malawi. I didn't sit in some office, classroom or coffee shop and ask what I wanted to do with my life. Life called to me, I got on the pitch, and actually *doing* something shaped what Emerging Leaders became.

So what would I say was the passionate purpose that drove me? In my instance I think it was a couple of things. First, the injustice of seeing that where you are born can limit your access to the best of everything. But also, recognising that people have amazing potential and that they need the best life leadership development, so they can lead themselves out of poverty. That is the purpose that kept me going from 2005 to 2020. That first trip to Zambia began to shape what I'm calling here a passionate purpose, or what others might call 'being gripped by something bigger than myself'. I'm also aware that it may not have been just one purpose for me for my whole life. I can see an evolving story over the decades, but there are consistent strands like fulfilling potential and how human transformation happens. I am having to ask the question all over again even as I write this to you.

Recently I listened to Robin Steinberg being interviewed by Chris Anderson,[39] the boss of TED talks. Robin and her husband founded an initiative called the Bail Project.[40] She saw so many issues caused by unconvicted people being put into the criminal justice system simply because they couldn't afford to pay the bail to keep them out of prison, even though many of them were eventually found not guilty. There was a point when Anderson asked Steinberg what motivated an extremely successful New York lawyer to begin this project helping criminals. Her answer took me aback, because it wasn't what I'd expected. She said, 'To be honest... it was anger.' As I reflected on her response, I realised that it wasn't so surprising after all. Injustice and anger sleep in the same bed. Mandela was angry. 'This is not OK' is probably one of the most common drivers to finding your bigger purpose, something larger than yourself. What the anger did for Steinberg was that she didn't need to *try* to become passionate about her new mission; anger *is* a passion. It's an energy that takes you past your inertia tipping point into doing something. For others, the driver might be joy, or grief, or pain. Overjoyed with the possibility of contributing something useful, hurt by what you've seen or what you or your loved ones have experienced – any strong emotion, positive or negative, can have the same effect as anger. They awaken in us a deeper, passionate purpose to do something. They drive us into action.

It seems to me that the call that starts any of us along the trail to a bigger purpose lies in questions like these: What makes you angry in the world? What grieves you? What motivates you? What wakes you up? What gives you joy? What gets under your skin? What need or opportunity have you seen that just won't go away? What do you feel the world needs from you, is asking of you? But it's easy to see these as just emotions, rather than clues or drivers to a passionate purpose.

I have a friend called Frances. She's a doctor and has worked in general practice, public health and leadership development within the UK's National Health Service. When I first heard her talking about issues of women's health, she sounded angry. Very angry. Especially about issues surrounding the opportunities for female healthcare professionals. She was angry at inequalities, angry at how people weren't squaring up either to the issues or to the opportunities to give women doctors equal chances in all aspects of healthcare. But she feared that people were put off by her anger. The more we talked, the more I realised there was something deeper going on within her. This wasn't just a rant, it was a vocation in the making, a bigger purpose wanting to be born from within her. As we continued to talk, we also began to reframe the anger as a passion for justice and a call to campaign for women health professionals and on women's health issues. She could use the anger as fuel to start fighting on women's behalf, which she did and ended up publishing a paper with the UN on gender equality.

When we feel pain or grief or anger about some value that is being violated, or some cause that needs championing, it's often what writer and speaker Bill Hybels calls a holy discontent,[41] because it almost has a spiritual dimension, a bigger self that is rising up within us. If I dare say it, it's almost like love breaks out. If love means going beyond ourselves to reach out to the needs or the life of others, then that strong emotion that drives us to something beyond or bigger than ourselves could be another way of seeing love in action.

It's so easy to look at Mandela's life from the perspective of the present rather than the past. We look back and see what now appears as a wonderfully crafted hero story. But that isn't the truth. When you read the story forward, from childhood to adulthood, you see a complicated journey. There were no straight roads or pretty endings when the story was actually being grown in his life. What I learned from him is that you begin right where you are and you lean into that.

It seems to me that finding that big why, discovering what the world needs from me, is often like living in a detective novel. The answer is there, but it's not in its fully formed shape, complete and ready to go. In my experience, it's often a gentle process of spotting the clues, taking them seriously and seeing where they take us next. Like a good detective story, the trail may have a lot of dead ends, but the secret is not to give up, to keep going, to continue searching. The journey of discovery will challenge you and shape you, lead you to add some ideas and drop others. That is the nature of becoming. It's a messy work of art, not an assembly line construction.

A few years ago I was delivering some training to workers in a garment factory in Bangalore, India. We had about fifty people in a sweaty basement room for four days. At the end of the training everyone was challenged to start a project that would either generate income or benefit their local community. We told people to start small, but do something to prove to themselves that they could indeed lead their own lives. A few months passed and we returned to train some trainers out of that initial group, in order to bring the training to many people at the factory. As we arrived to set up, not knowing who from that original group had been selected to be trained to become a trainer, one diminutive woman sidled up to me and said, 'I did my project.'

'Excuse me?'

'I did my project. Like you asked us.'

'Great! What was the project?'

Her reply was totally unexpected: 'I got my street resurfaced with tarmac and now I am working on getting traffic lights put at the junction with the main road at the end.'

She quietly explained what I had heard from other conversations, that potholes in India kill people, they are a death trap. Cyclists would literally fall into potholes, or they would bump into a hole, wobble and lose control, and be hit by an oncoming car. This woman had witnessed these tragedies multiple times over the years and like everyone else had felt powerless to do anything about it. She would say to herself, 'What could I do? Why doesn't the government do something here?'

For some reason the challenge to do a project at the end of the training had sparked off a passion for a bigger purpose in her life. 'Why not me?' This was the new question she was asking herself. Linked to her anger and frustration about the pothole problem came a new thought. She became captivated by the possibility that she could do something. Over the following weeks she gathered her neighbours, got their agreement about taking action, formed a committee, came up with a strategy, lobbied the council, finally managed to get a representative of the council to come out to see the problem, explained how it could be solved and what kind of help the community could supply. Within a few months the whole road was tarmacked. Unbelievable! I've trained thousands of people over the years and seen countless different projects started, but this was a new one on me. This quiet, unassuming woman had achieved what even her own local government hadn't been able to get done.

She made me think of another woman, Andiswa, from one of Cape Town's townships. She had been depressed and wasn't working or getting out to meet people. A friend persuaded her to attend a training one of our teams was running and as a result Andiswa woke up to the fact that there were hordes of children wandering the streets and not in school. They had always been there, but she hadn't seen, or been able to see, what was in front of her eyes. The needs of these children and the idea that she could start something to help them captivated her. So she invited them into her front room and taught them a child-friendly version of what she had learned herself. The numbers grew and she converted her garage into a classroom. She now has a thriving afterschool club that keeps children off the gang-ridden streets of her community.

What do these stories stir in me? Apart from the need to let life get to me and prompt some kind of response, stimulate some passionate purpose, I need to lean into it, because passionate purpose is never delivered as a fully formed conviction. It grows. It needs to be shaped by the trials and challenges, the success and failures, of trying to take that idea forwards. One thing that going back and back and back to Africa over the years has shown me is the need to keep on feeding that flame. Once the fire is burning, the bigger idea, the passionate purpose – call it what you will – once that starts moving you in a direction, then you need to keep on feeding it. I found that as well as revisiting the places where the needs were that had originally got me on to the pitch, I could read books and articles and listen to talks that were relevant to the needs I was seeing. All of these helped to keep the flame alive.

For me, one of the hardest things at the start was the feeling that I knew less than nothing about poverty, Africa, HIV – anything. But I just kept telling myself, 'Stick with the passionate purpose, let that fuel you, start where you are, start small, do something, do one thing, build the idea brick on brick. Just keep on building.'

One thing I do know is that developing a passionate purpose is totally doable, but it can be scary. It was far easier to stay in the world I knew, which was safe and undemanding. I'd shaped my identity by being part of that safe place and if I stepped out of it then it wasn't just that I didn't know what to *do*, it was that I didn't know who I *was* in this new space.

Time has taught me that there is another, larger risk too. It's the risk of doing nothing – of staying, of shrinking or stagnating, of getting older but not wiser, of lingering too long. You could argue that stepping up, or stepping out, makes us a bigger person. You could argue that you become 'more you' than before. There are risks both ways: risks in stepping out and risks in staying put. Doing something has the risk of failure or burnout, and doing nothing has the risks of shrinking, feeling like you're marking time, being less than you could have been, reminiscing over wasted dreams, dying before you die. A hero is simply someone who gives themselves to something bigger than themselves.[42]

Dawna Markova's[43] famous poem opens with the same kind of purpose that Mandela displayed: 'I will not die an unlived life.'

Once those words have soaked in, we can discuss this further. Anyway, I look forward to seeing you both on Sunday.

Much love

Dad

STARTING A CONVERSATION

---

1. What makes you angry in the world? What grieves you? What motivates you? What wakes you up? What gives you joy? What gets under your skin? What need or opportunity have you seen that just won't go away? What do you feel the world needs from you, is asking of you?
2. If you described what the passionate purpose of your life is, what would you say? How is that demonstrated in your life right now?
3. Where can you begin to do something small, anything, to speak into the need that has caught your attention?

---

6. Intention – make it happen

Hi guys

What a great debate I've had with both of you this past week. It's so good that we were able to start it together and then continue it online. It's a weird thing being a parent, especially when your children get to be young adults. You still want to hold on to everything you enjoyed when your children were younger. You guys have your own independent lives to live and yet we are still all timelessly connected.

I want to follow up on your questions about how people develop into who they eventually become. I think I touched on some of my thoughts in my last letter, but it's worth developing them a bit more. As soon as we wake up in the morning, life is knocking at our door and every day it is different. Despite any similarities, every day is definitely *not* Groundhog Day. One day I woke up and I had a cancer diagnosis; another day I woke up and I was asked to go to Kenya; and on another day I was taken on a visit into the backstreets of Chennai to be introduced to an ancient community of weapon makers to the kings of old. I know these are slightly extreme examples, but every day pitches something at us. Two days ago, I had to pull a project that I had been trying to land for many months in Rwanda. Yesterday, a person we thought we would employ for a role in the organisation changed her mind and decided she didn't want to join us.

If you asked a child where they go to learn, they would reply, 'Every day I go to school and learning happens in the classroom.' Well, life is the classroom for becoming our version of Mandela. What he experienced as a child, or in his law practice, or the first time he met Walter Sisulu, all presented him with opportunities, choices, pressures and encouragements. It was Sisulu who saw Mandela's leadership potential. What if they hadn't met? What if life had thrown Mandela a different ball? It is easy to think that people like him went to some special school for super-heroes, but the truth is that the classroom of life is the same for us all. Life presents us with the growth opportunities each moment of each day. It's what we do with these moments that shapes us. Every moment is a moment to ask: 'What can this teach me and who do I want to become as a result of it?'

On Robben Island, one day the prisoners were forced to take a pile of rocks from one side of the island to the other. Why? For no reason other than the cruel-mindedness of the guards. It was back-breaking, sun-scorching work, but they completed what was asked of them. Their guards then told them that they now had to take those same rocks all the way back to the other side of the island. Naturally the prisoners were furious, but Mandela turned it into a classroom for character building. He encouraged his fellow prisoners to see the opportunity for developing a different kind of character and demonstrating it to the guards. Life threw the circumstances at him, but the choice of who he would become was in Mandela's response. This approach is embedded deeply in all the spiritual and meaningful views of life. 'What can this teach me?' is the wise response to everything.

When life is the classroom, then everything is our teacher.

I think that what I want to say – and maybe I'm communicating it badly – is that it is so easy to view Mandela as a hero. We all love heroes. We love to put people up on pedestals. But then they become an inspiration and a discouragement at the same time. Being a hero is unattainable for the majority of the population and that is the opposite of what I'm trying to say here. Of course Mandela was unique, but the qualities that we revere him for can be learned by anyone. By my response to life as a classroom, I can develop the same qualities in my life that he developed. It's not the hero Mandela that I want to focus on, but rather me and you. Becoming Mandela simply means becoming fully me and fully equipped with the qualities that he demonstrated for all of us. Just as he grew those qualities over a lifetime, so can I – and so can you.

It starts with intentionality. If life is a classroom then we are all in it, no exceptions. That means we all have daily opportunities to grow, to become. Mandela was intentional about his growth. It undergirded all of his responses to life. I too can be intentional with how I respond to everything that happens in my life's classroom. A good life doesn't happen by accident. This means that a good life happens intentionally. It happens when I say to myself, 'I know who I want to become and I'm going to use today to help me become that person.'

I was talking with your cousin Anya the other week. We were sitting in her front room chilling out with her hubby and the dog, eating flapjacks. The scene was relaxed and trusting, which probably allowed her to open up about becoming a mum for the first time. She talked about being both excited and terrified in equal measure. She was terrified that she wouldn't find a mummy-groove within herself when the baby actually arrived. She started being very honest about the deep questions of her life: 'Is there more to life than what I see in front of me? Why am I here? What is my purpose?' Great questions. Deep questions. Important questions. We talked about her getting hold of a journal and writing her heart out in her own exploration of what was going on inside her head at this time. Life had thrown her a classroom called 'pregnancy' and she was responding to the lessons being offered to her.

You both have been there recently. You've both had the overwhelming experience of this awesome miracle of a new life and know so well all of the thoughts and questions it throws up within you. Anya knew she was standing on this amazing, perplexing, scary, joyful threshold. She said that she thought the journaling idea was a great one, but as I got up and headed off, I was quietly wondering to myself, 'Will she do it? Will she actually make the time to write about her experiences and questions, switch off her phone and go for it? Will she be intentional?'

The reason I was wondering this is that I know for myself just how hard it is to get started on something. I knew for ages that I should practise meditation, but it took a definite intention to get started.

Good intentions are different to intentionality. Good intentions are like new year's resolutions. I've given up on good intentions like that, because I know I won't do them for long. Remember the friends that you brought over to ours for the new year celebration last year? They were a great crowd and it was fun to fill the house with their enthusiasm. I'm not sure if you were there, but over breakfast on New Year's Day, I casually asked one of your friends what her new year's resolutions were and her reply encouraged me to think differently. She started by saying she had stopped making new year's resolutions for the same reasons I had. They were a waste of time. They never happened. What she then said was different, though. She said, 'I've been practising whole year values.' That got my attention, so I quizzed her further.

She explained: 'What I do now is just decide on a value that I want to be true of me this year (who I want to become) and each day I just think about it, reflect on it and I find simple actions that embody it. Then, I quietly celebrate to myself if I do something that I think fits that value.'

'For example?' I asked.

'Take kindness. I want to be a kinder person by the end of this year. I know it's a great thought, but if I leave it as a thought then it won't happen. So, I get intentional each day and look for opportunities, in the events of the day, to practise kindness.'

After a pause, she summed it up by saying, 'Yep, I just choose one value, and I do it.'

As far as I can see, intentionality is simply saying 'I'm going to do this and so I'll take the next step, however small.'

I remember the first time I came across the work of Goethe. A friend introduced me to him at a time when I was dithering. I was talking a lot about changing my career, but I wasn't doing it. I was in new year's resolution, good intentions mode, not intentionality mode. He showed me this quote:

> Until one is committed, there is hesitancy, the chance to draw back. Concerning all acts of initiative (and creation), there is one elementary truth that ignorance of which kills countless ideas and splendid plans: that the moment one definitely

> commits oneself, then Providence moves too. All sorts of things occur to help one that would never otherwise have occurred. A whole stream of events issues from the decision, raising in one's favor all manner of unforeseen incidents and meetings and material assistance, which no man could have dreamed would have come his way. I learned a deep respect for one of Goethe's couplets:
>
> Whatever you can do or dream you can, begin it.
> Boldness has genius, power and magic in it![44]

There is power in action – that's what I discovered. Just do it. Take the first step. You don't need to know all of the steps, or the shape of the journey. Just begin.

There was a time in prison when Mandela started learning Afrikaans, the language of his white oppressors, and he encouraged his fellow prisoners to do the same. Some of his colleagues were really angry with him and accused him of giving in to the enemy; he was learning the oppressive white man's language! Others thought that, given he was in prison for life, it was simply a waste of time. But Mandela had his eye on who he was becoming, not who he was, and he told his friends that they needed to take the longer view. He told them that when they were released (they had been told they would die in prison), if they were to negotiate a different future then they would need to understand white people's thinking, their history, their views on life, their very thought processes. He said:

> If you talk to a man in a language he understands, that goes to his head. If you talk to him in *his* language, that goes to his heart.[45]

Mandela spoke to his guards in Afrikaans, was able to negotiate with de Klerk in Afrikaans, could speak to the fears of Afrikaners in their own language, because he was intentional right from the start of his prison sentence. Not only did he learn the language of his oppressors, he started a university, pursued a ruthless regime of kindness towards his guards, was rigorous in his physical exercise, had a hunger for devouring knowledge, chose to forgive, practised the daily self-evaluation of his character. And all of these things started with a first step, with intentionality. A first question, a first page of a book read, a first meditation session in his cell, a first lesson in Afrikaans. He just began. Against the threat of death and hopelessness, he began. Intentionality was like the mechanism that connected the engine of his life's purpose to the actions of his life. Intentionality releases the power into the legs, or the mouth, or the hand, or the mind.

As you both know, one of my favourite poems by Dawna Markova[46] is a poem of intentionality. I quoted you the first line in the last letter. It starts like this:

> I will not die an unlived life
> I will not live in fear
> of falling or catching fire.
> I choose to inhabit my days...

And further on

> I choose to risk my significance;
> to live...

It's a poem of intent, of choice, of action:

> I will...
> I will not...
> I choose...

Like you, I keep wondering what the X factor is. What is it that nudges me over the line from new year's resolution mode into intentionality mode? What nudges me over the line from 'I will not die an unlived life' to actually inhabiting today?

I think I may have told you this story before; I can't remember. Anyway, when I was in my final year at school, a group of us eighteen-year-olds excitedly planned a great tour of Europe to celebrate the end of exams. The school library was Mission Control where we held our ambitious planning sessions, maps laid out on grey-topped library tables, engraved with initials by bored past students. We hatched a plan, including a rough route, and then discussed what the best type of travel would be. Student rail cards or not? Youth hostels or cheap pensions? (Airbnb didn't exist in those days.) Then I distinctly remember that period, from Easter up to exam time in June, when one by one people's enthusiasm began to wane and one by one my friends dropped out. Bill had to get a job. Jenny's parents weren't happy. Fatima's parents were offering an exciting holiday in the Caribbean. I remember being genuinely shocked when I realised that most of our planning conversations had been pure hubris. I felt like someone had told a joke and I was the only one in the group who didn't understand it was funny. But I was determined not to give up and to follow through on my intentionality. So the day after my final exams, I jumped on a train in London alone, headed to the coast, caught a ferry to Europe and did my own version of the grand tour through France and Switzerland.

What I keep asking myself is what determines the difference between dreams and intentionality? In the case of this grand tour, was it fear? And fear of what? The unknown? Being attacked in the backstreets of Paris? Was it the realisation of the financial cost? Was it the dawning reality that the summer needed to be spent earning money to pay for university if the grades turned out OK?

One thing that has helped me a lot – and you will definitely have heard me say this before – is that if you want to say *no* to something, then you need to have a bigger *yes*. If I want to say no to fear, to inertia, to staying still, then I need something that I want even more. What was Mandela's bigger *yes*? His famous words at the Rivonia trial, where he was sentenced to life imprisonment, reveal the answer. I quoted them in a previous letter, but they are worth repeating here:

> I have cherished the ideal of a democratic and free society in which all persons live together in harmony and with equal opportunities. It is an ideal which I hope to live for and to achieve. But if needs be, it is an ideal for which I am prepared to die.[47]

He wanted something more than a comfortable life or things remaining as they were. I think Mandela's Rivonia speech reveals something else about intentionality too. Lots of people wanted Apartheid to end, just as lots of people wanted Brexit to happen or not happen, action on the climate crisis, an end to gun or knife crime, or whatever. People retweet until they are blue in the fingers, but that doesn't mean they do anything at all. I think the bigger yes has *really* got to matter to you, not just *idealistically* matter. You have to be at a place where you can't tolerate yourself, or the situation, any more: 'This has to change; this is what I must make happen; whatever it takes I need to do something.' So there is something about having a deep conviction that means you can't *not* do something. You *have* to do it. Doing something is more important than doing nothing, than staying where you are. Even if, as in the case of Mandela, it means being prepared to die for it.

Once there's something bigger, something that has caught our vision and attention enough to be able to say no to whatever might stop it, whether it's an activity or developing a part of my character – then what?

I once saw the famous golfer Nick Faldo playing at a world-ranking event. As soon as he'd finished his round, instead of returning to the clubhouse for a hot shower and a beer, he walked straight over to the practice ground with his coach and for the next few hours practised, practised and practised some more. That's called discipline. This is what turns the intention into action. I know the word discipline doesn't always have much appeal, but I was helped by discovering that its root comes from the Greek word for gymnasium. Both of you boys know what it means to train every day to run a half-marathon or cycle road races. The sports gymnasium, or life's gymnasium, is a metaphor for that place you go to day after day after day to repeat little actions in order to develop muscle that enables you to do the important things, to achieve your aims.

Recently, reflecting on how the angry young man became the empathic elder and leader, I found myself having a conversation with myself and saying, 'OK, Trevor. Enough is enough. You can read these books as many times as you like and admire what Mandela changed in himself, but what one character trait do you want to change in yourself? Choose just one.'

So I made a list of things about myself that I would like to be said of me when I was eighty years old and then I chose one: humility. I could see the pride and defensiveness in myself and the myriad ways it showed up. So began a painful journey that still continues. Talking, journaling, getting feedback, scraping myself off the floor, being pulled back to self-honesty. Facing down my ego, my oversensitivity to criticism, wanting to look amazing, wanting to make stories more impressive than they really were – it's been tough and it's not a journey you can make alone. But it's felt like I have started a journey towards becoming my version of Mandela in one important area of my life, because I finally got intentional. I just keep reminding myself that as the saying goes, 'a good life doesn't happen by accident'.

What I'm trying to say is well captured by Nancy Hollander, a civil rights and criminal defence lawyer most famous for her work on behalf of prisoners at Guantanamo Bay. She is also a jiu-jitsu practitioner, by both exercise and nature. When asked what her life advice to people would be she said:

> Whatever you do, do it with intent. Just one good kick and one good punch is better than twenty you didn't have any intent behind. Don't do something unless you mean it, don't do something unless you are committed.[48]

I hope all this makes some sense to you in terms of how I am seeking to learn one of these Mandela-type attributes.

'Whatever you do, do it with intent.' So simple.

With love

Dad

STARTING A CONVERSATION

1. Where do you feel you demonstrate good intentionality and where do you not do so?
2. How do you take a word like 'discipline' and make it attractive in your own life?
3. Talk about the areas of your life that you want to be more intentional about.

7. Aspiration – get out of your own way

Hi guys

I'm glad you got the chance to meet Robert the other night when you came round on your way south. It's great to have such good neighbours. What I obviously didn't tell you was that after you'd left, he started asking about our work with Emerging Leaders and he made some comment about how wonderful and amazing it was to make such an impact on so many lives. What then happened would have been funny if it hadn't been so sad. In response to his kind words, I started to say 'actually we've trained over 85,000 people since we started'. Thankfully he and Jane had already begun a different conversation and so my words were lost before I'd had the chance to complete my sentence. As they talked, I found myself waiting for a pause so I could jump in again and finish what I was going to say, but the conversation had moved on and I was now asking myself why I felt I needed to say those figures anyway. For whose benefit? Had something been lacking from the conversation we'd been having?

I realised I was about to speak out entirely for my own grandstanding benefit. Disguised as a humble sharing of information, it was pure ego-centredness. When you catch your own self-importance red handed, it really is ugly. And why did I need to tell you the numbers in this letter? Did it add anything, or did I want you to think, 'Wow, what you are doing is so cool, you are such an amazing dad'? Dads' egos are as needy as their sons'. The needs of the ego are a bear trap in my own front yard.

My unpleasant encounter with myself encouraged me to follow up on something I talked about before. You remember I told you in a previous letter how Mandela never lost his respect for the elders from his youth. He listened to them when he was young, he listened to them when he was old, and he even created a group of global elders in his later years. I've been wondering what it was about these olders that made them what he and tradition have named *elders*? As I said before, we are all getting older (I'm obviously and understandably more aware of that fact than you), but older isn't the same as elder. What's the difference? Older is simply accumulating the years, but elders accumulate wisdom, gravitas and perspective, and they have something that young people want and need. They offer themselves as a compass to help younger people navigate their own becoming. So, in asking myself what the difference is, the next obvious question is: How do I shift from just getting older to becoming an elder, becoming my own version of Mandela? (Stick with me, there is a connection with ego.)

Well, I think I found a clue recently, when I discovered a phrase about eldership in the ancient wisdom literature of the Bible. It says, 'Anyone who aspires to become an elder, desires a good work.' What really interested me there was this word *aspires*. As I looked at it closely, I found out a couple of things. The word itself means to reach or stretch out, which I guess shows that it needs me to make an effort, to desire, to want to get somewhere (intentionality). As we grow older, starting at whatever age you or I are now, we need to *want* to become this elder and not just get older. I then realised that the word *aspire* is in the middle voice (there are passive, active and middle voices in grammar), which means that I make this effort in response to something bigger or beyond myself (what we talked about in a previous letter when I wrote about having purpose). But the real kicker is in the word itself. The Greek word translated as aspire is ὀρέγω (orego). You will have seen the clue already in the two parts of the word orego: 'or', to get beyond, and 'ego'. To aspire is to get beyond, to stretch beyond your own ego. So in essence, that insight from the Bible is saying:

> Hey, if you want to become a Mandela in your own backyard, then that's great, but to do so means you have to a bigger 'yes' for your life and actively get beyond your own ego-centredness. That's the hard work you're going to have to do on yourself.

To be an elder we need to work on getting beyond our self. 'Get over yourself', as you often hear people say.

The story of Scott Harrison is a great example of this. He is the founder and CEO of Charity Water,[49] which aims to get clean water to everyone in the world who doesn't have it. (Yes, a huge vision, but he's hit 8.5 million users so far!) He spent ten years feeding his ego and building a Scott-centred empire, which meant he had every house, car, woman, drink, drugs and acclaim that the ego could feed on to make it feel good. Except it didn't. At the height of his self-confessed hedonism, he had a realisation one night that however much he fed his ego, it would never be enough. From that wake-up moment he decided to create a life that was 180 degrees opposite from the life he had been living. To do that he tried to stop the drink, the drugs, the smoking, the pornography and the gambling, but with limited effect. That is how it was until the day he decided to get on a ship run by the charity Mercy Ships,[50] who take doctors, nurses and surgeons to places in the world that have little to zero medical help. Harrison could see that the staff were motivated by a cause that was bigger than themselves. He describes walking up the gangplank onto the ship and how in that very moment he knew he was stepping into the bigger *yes* of his life, and never again did he touch the things that fed his inner hunger. He *aspired* to be someone different than he currently was and so he stepped beyond his ego-centred self in response to a larger purpose for his life. (I'm not suggesting that this was his last battle with his ego – but it was the crucial first battle.)

Ego isn't a very pleasant word most of the time, but it also gets a bad press. I said last time I wrote that we are born ego-centric. It's not something wrong, it's totally normal. We need the scaffolding of our ego to get going in life. The problem arises when we start growing physically, but allow the ego to remain at the *centre* of who we are.

Imagine arriving in your early twenties or thirties and you look up to the horizon and see who you are becoming and then intentionally create a vision of who you *could* become. While you are looking across the fields to that new vision of who you could become, you realise that there is this big wall in front of you that you need to get over first, if you are to make the journey of becoming. The wall in front of you is called ego-centredness. We all have the challenge, or opportunity, to get over it, or beyond it, to become the person we want to become.

As our ego is developing, it needs to pose some important life questions:

- How do I get noticed here so I feel admired or valued?
- How do I feel safe around here, when there is so much uncertainty?
- How do I live forever, rather than cease to exist?
- How do I get respected by others?'

How we grapple and discover answers to these huge questions can leave our ego feeling safe and secure and valued, or it can leave us feeling vulnerable, fragile, raw, in pain or fearful at a deep level. Of course, the negative feelings are not ones that any of us want, so we then need to develop ways of keeping ourselves feeling good, feeling safe, feeling respected. (We call these ego defences.)

So this ego of ours is very alive and attuned to what it needs and extremely good at finding ways of getting it. Priest Richard Rohr says the ego will put up with almost anything, even death, rather than surrender its defences, its familiar ways of getting through life. Naturally, all of this internal wrestling going on inside of me then plays out in all of my relationships at work, with family, friends, at the local shop, or wherever. The big issue here is that if I want to become a bigger person, with a bigger purpose that is greater than my ego-centric self, then I have to do something with *me*, because my ego only wants to keep me as I am.

There's a problem here. I'm not saying you have to throw the ego out of the window of your life's journey, but I am saying it will limit who you become if you don't learn to keep it firmly in the back seat, with its hands off the steering wheel.

To be honest, I've struggled with ego-centredness all of my adult life. I don't mean I've been parading myself everywhere in a noisy way, I think for me it's been a lot subtler than that. I can see how wanting recognition and respect, or feeling overly bruised by criticism, has been the undercurrent in many of my interactions.

At work, I once set myself a challenge to closely observe my ego in action over a month. I spotted more than ten different ways in which my fragile ego could be affecting the way I led my teams.

This is a hard conversation to have with you both. I want you to think your dad has got his s**t together, to be a man you are proud of. I don't want you, or anyone for that matter, seeing the truth of me wrestling with my ego. I want you to think of me as great, not average, because average people don't get noticed. That is my ego crying out to be noticed! When you used to cover your face as a kid, you thought that because you couldn't see me, I couldn't see you. You would squeal 'You can't see me', but of course I could. It was only you who thought I couldn't. I guess that's how it is with all this difficult stuff. People probably can see us a lot better than we see ourselves.

Mandela was very clear on the need for courageous friends around him, who could mirror back to him what flaws they were seeing in his character:

> Walter (Sisulu) and Kathy (Ahmed Kathrada) share one common feature which forms an essential part of our friendship and which I value very much – they never hesitate to criticize me for my mistakes and throughout my political career have served as a mirror through which I can see myself.[51]

I mentioned that phrase 'get over yourself', but how on earth do you or I do that? For me the hardest part has been learning to spot my ego in action. My ego is so clever: it's like a chameleon that changes colour so as not to be spotted. It took me years to be able to admit to myself that I don't like criticism, or being told what to do in an area in which I feel experienced. My defences kick in so instinctively that I often don't spot the underlying feelings of shame or vulnerability. It's like I developed a hyper-alert radar system early on in life, which could pick up perceived criticism at a hundred metres. Fixing this is a painfully slow process, aided greatly by having someone alongside me who I know both loves me and has the courage to speak up and tell me what they see. (Jane won't let me play 'you can't see me'.) To be honest, having someone give you feedback is both the best and the hardest thing to live with, but without the honest feedback the chameleon-ego would just keep on playing its tricks.

I'm slowly learning to pay attention to my reactions too. The reactions have always been there, but I don't think I paid them the right kind of respect. What I've realised is that my anger, my irritation, my anxieties, my frustrations, are all simply my defensive reactions to my ego feeling under threat.

I sat in a meeting yesterday and everyone was debating some issue and I couldn't get a word into the conversation. I felt frustrated, then I felt irritated, but this time I managed to have a chat with myself privately and ask, 'What's going on here?' I didn't like the answer I heard: 'I've got a great idea and no one is asking me, or inviting me, to get it on the table and *I'm* the guy whose been around the longest.' Yuk.

The ego does feel pretty ugly when it's exposed. But at least it then gives me choices. Like with Robert the other night, once I'd seen it, I had a choice. I could make sure I forced my great statistics into the conversation, or I could choose to stay quiet and let others talk. I think Stephen Covey used to call it *finding the gap* – the gap between stimulus and response. With my untamed ego there was no gap. Someone would speak or do something (stimulus) and I would shoot straight back with a *yes, but...* (response). *Yes, buts* are so unsubtle, when it comes to my ego's defences. Spotting the feeling in me and then having a gap between that feeling and making a response is where I get to see that there are choices.

There is no easy way of saying this to me, or to you, but it's a straight fact that to become who I, or you, want to be, we have to do hard work on ourselves and that hard work is the daily work of a lifetime. When I was cycle racing in my late teens, I loved the racing, but the real work happened in the daily training sessions. The same is true of working on ourselves: we want to be effective, we want outcomes, results at home, or work, or wherever, but that only comes in a lasting way if we do the hard work on ourselves each day. AA[52] has always said that to make a change, to create transformation in yourself, you have to take a personal, searching and fearless moral inventory. Gosh, that's tough.

The best way I can describe getting over that ego wall is to see it like a garden (sorry to mix the metaphors). A garden grows flowers, but it also grows weeds, and no matter how hard you work at pulling up weeds, they grow again. It's hard, until you accept that this is how it is. Then you just weed your garden every day, because that is what is needed. I think the same is true of the ego. The weeds need pulling up every day. I'm never going to get rid of my ego defences, but I can be alert to them, manage them, limit them; I can make room for better choices. Often the deeper, unfaced, unhealed parts of ourselves create this hole inside of us that we need to fill. There can sometimes be a scary, empty, lonely place that is hard to own up to.

I've been reading Samantha Power's[53] autobiography and she talks about the way she avoided her deep inner hurt and loneliness, which was by avoiding letting anyone get too close to her. She would get so far and then sabotage the relationship. Therapy was certainly crucial for her, as it has been for me. Therapy is good for looking at the healing of the damaged ego – where painful things from the past have hurt us and we try to fix the hurt ourselves, through other people, our work etc. Personally, therapy provided a safe space to take a hard look at my insecure ego and make friends with it; to realise that I would still survive if I were honest about my needs and defences. I guess therapy was like bringing into the light of a personal relationship those parts of me that I was hiding from myself and others (though I think I was kidding myself if I think others didn't see my vulnerabilities).

Meditation has also been a lifesaver for me. The daily process of quieting down my busy head, looking at what has been going on, making room for some new thoughts and fresh choices has also been invaluable. I know we spoke about meditation recently, but I definitely think it's worth pursuing and trying for a period of time... not just a day or two! One of my greatest regrets in life is that I didn't really get into meditation until my mid-fifties. I would definitely change that if I could do it all over again.

I realise this letter may have seemed a little more introspective, but I didn't want to run from that. Anyway, the word introspective means 'to take a look inside'. That inner look is definitely worth it, because I've seen only too painfully that when I haven't dealt with the issues in the inner theatre of my life, then they just get enacted on the outside stage, and that won't get any of us over that wall and down that field to the horizon, to becoming our version of Mandela.

Let me close with a little moment of Mandela's own history. In 1998 he took President Clinton personally around Robben Island. Clinton was awed by seeing at first hand what Mandela had endured.

'Surely,' Clinton said, 'you must have felt some anger and the need for retribution after all this?'

Mandela's answer?

> No. If I had allowed myself those thoughts, I would have remained in prison, but it would have been a prison of my own making.

This was his lesson to us all. Do the hard work on yourself. Win the inner victory over your ego, if you are going to win any outer victories in life. What is the inner victory? To be honest, I think it is getting to a more resourceful, at-peace place with ourselves, a place where we can love ourselves. This is definitely something we should talk more about some time.

I'm going to try to swing by your way when we are in Oxford next Monday, but let's keep on talking anyway.

Love

Dad

STARTING A CONVERSATION

---

1. Where can you spot your areas of greatest ego vulnerability?
2. If you took one area of your ego to work one, what would it be and what could you do to keep it 'in the back seat' rather than controlling your life choices and responses?
3. Who is, or could be, on your personal 'team' – people who you trust and who are willing to give you honest feedback?

---

8. Inspiration – breathe out what you breathe in

Hi guys

I would like to take up your question, the one you raised when we spoke on the phone. You mentioned that Mandela was truly inspiring, but you also thought it's unrealistic to think that we can all be like him. I want to challenge that thought, or at least attempt to shape it a little. I think we label Mandela as very inspiring because there were so many things about him that engage and motivate us. His courage, his wisdom, his empathy, his passion, his mission, his shirts (just kidding), his gravitas, his moral authority – all of these different qualities are inspiring. That's why he stood out. However, I do think we can all be inspiring, in at least one or two of these ways. Where I agree with you is that to be seen as inspiring is a judgement that only others can make of you. If I said to you that I think I'm inspiring, that would probably prove I wasn't, that I was being at best aspirational and at worst egotistical. Being inspiring is the visible outcome and we can't control it, but we can make the investments that will lead to us being inspiring.

Let me back up a bit and try to define what exactly inspiration means. In all of the leadership training I've run over the years, whenever I asked for a brainstorm on the characteristics of great leaders, the one word that would surface every single time was 'inspiring'. Great leaders are inspiring. It was this revelation that set me thinking so much about this whole issue.

Of course, the meaning of the word 'inspire' is literally 'to breathe in'. If we don't inspire (breathe in), we die. Inspiration is the basic 'food' of life. We breathe, fish breathe, trees breathe and birds breathe. Breathing is core to all organic life. There is a version of breathing that sits in the middle point between breathing and not breathing and it's called shallow breathing, or breathing in old, stale air. You're alive, but hardly thriving. That was my aha moment, because I realised that the reason Mandela is inspiring is because he was committed to breathing in new, fresh air. He was always learning, always pursuing wisdom, always growing his courage, always practising his empathy (breathing in, inspiring). And all he breathed in, he breathed out, in all his actions and his words. He was inspiring others because he was always inspiring himself. We say 'Mandela was inspiring' because we have experienced his words and actions breathing life into us in some way. If this is what being inspiring is, then we can all become inspiring. It can be learned.

Mandela actually saw himself as a very ordinary man. In a talk he gave at the London School of Economics, he said:

> My inspirations are men and women who have emerged throughout the globe and who have chosen the world as the theatre of their operations and who fight socio-economic conditions which do not help towards the advancement of humanity, wherever that occurs. Men and women who fight the suppression of the human voice, who fight disease, illiteracy, ignorance, poverty and hunger. Some are known, others are not. These are the people who have inspired me.[54]

What I learned from this is to start by asking myself who inspires me and why. When I really stopped to think about it, there have been so many people I could say this about. As Mandela noted, some are well known and others not. One of the hidden ones for me was called George Roberts. Long before you guys were born, in fact before I was even married, I was involved in community youth work. One Saturday, a group of us went to a day conference in North Norfolk, at a centre called Pickenham. It was a two-hour drive from where I lived and seemed like it was in the middle of nowhere. I can't remember anything about the day at all, but I can still recall what happened after the conference concluded. Everyone went off home, but for some reason we had to hang around and so a couple of our group, me included, went to the main lounge. There were two people there. One greeted us and the other was quietly reading in the corner of the room. We started chatting with the guy who greeted us about what we had been learning that day and what we did back home with our youth group. After a few minutes he pointed to the guy in the corner of the room and said, 'He's the person you should be talking to; you should ask him to tell you his story.'

So we did. And George Roberts' story was remarkable. He had been a missionary in Uganda at the time of Idi Amin. As things began to get threatening, more and more expats and missionaries left the country. In the end they all had to go, or get thrown out, or be killed. George's organisation back in the UK demanded that he leave immediately, for his own safety. But he decided to stay. He had lived with the villagers he had been working with for years and love and trust had grown between them. How could he abandon them for his own safety's sake? He was one of the only missionaries, if not the only one, to stay in Uganda during the full terrors of the Amin regime. Amazingly, he survived and here he was, an unknown hero, sitting drinking afternoon tea in a remote part of England. Why do I remember him to this day? Because he inspired me. His courage, his love for the people, his humility and quiet spirit, all spoke volumes in that brief encounter. They all breathed life into me, in a way that has stayed with me for over forty years.

I'd love to know who inspires you guys. If you have a moment, write and tell me. When I made my own list, as well as Mandela I had cycling heroes from my youth like Tom Simpson and Eddy Merckx or Tony Gowland; Paul Tournier of course, and Eddie Vass; Peter Wiegand and Lutz Ketwig, who I worked with in international youth work in Austria; Edith Eger, Rabbi Nahum Ward-Lev. My list grew and grew. Why were they all inspiring? Some aspect of who *they* were lit up a possibility for some aspect of *me*.

Maybe their discipline inspires me to better discipline, their dedication to be more dedication, their empathy to be more empathic, the way they broke through their own limiting beliefs to break through my own, or their courage to be more courageous in my own growth. It could be their insight, physical courage, moral courage, wisdom, skill, knowledge or creativity. Anything. But it pushes some button in me – it creates some fresher air for me to breathe.

As I think about what it means to be inspiring, I have an image in my mind. I don't know if it will help you, but it helps me, so let's try it. You know when you are walking along and suddenly your nostrils are hit by some new, unexpected scent? The reflex is to stop breathing, to stop inhaling. It's like the brain registers the unfamiliar smell and issues an instant warning. So you turn away or turn off the smell. The brain then does the analysis and says, 'Actually that smell was OK; danger over.' But by then you have moved on. This is what the analogy means to me. When I note that someone is inspiring me in any way, large or small, I shouldn't turn away, but rather I should lean in – actually lean in to the inspiration and let it fully do its work. Let the feeling of inspiration really get to me. Wake me up. Illuminate me. Prod me to ask myself why it is inspiring. What is this person inspiring me to be or do?

When I'm inspired there's a feeling of being lit up, enlarged in some way, captured by possibilities. There are two possible outcomes. The first is to ignore it and move on, and the second is to let it inspire me to action, to doing something. For example, I can allow Desmond Tutu's courage to speak truth to power to give me the courage to speak up about some injustice I see around me. Or as I listen to the writer Elizabeth Gilbert speak, I can let it inspire me to own my own potential as a writer, the possibilities for who I could become. I can allow other people to enlarge me. It is like their inspiration reveals to me who I *could* become, gives me an agenda for my own growth possibilities, and I can take action to step into that person's example and make it my own. Inspiration helps me grow into my potential.

Majd Mashharawi[55] is someone who inspires me. She invented a way of making bricks out of the ashes of bombed buildings in Gaza, to create new buildings for displaced people to live in. She had about 150 attempts and failures before she got the design right. She inspires me not to give up on a good idea just because it doesn't succeed the first few times. She inspires me to develop courage when the context makes me fearful. She inspires me to look at what is lying around me through new eyes of possibility.

I always think of the line in Dawna Markova's poem 'I Will Not Die an Unlived Life', where she talks about choosing to 'allow my living to open me'. For me this is the key to inspiration: that we allow people to open us up to the inspiration to be a bigger person than we would have been without them. If we don't keep on growing, then we will become smaller and, dare I say it, more trivial. (I speak particularly of people my age, who seem to be already settling rather than growing.)

What am I doing to nurture the possibility of becoming more inspiring to others? I keep on breathing in any kind of life – reading, meditation, time spent thinking and processing to gain wisdom, looking at things in nature that create a sense of awe, stretching my courage, pushing in to issues of injustice. When I heard the news that I had prostate cancer, what I remember was being inspired by the fact that Mandela, Desmond Tutu and Richard Rohr had all journeyed through that diagnosis and continued to grow as influential people. Their attitude and courage gave me a better attitude and courage towards what lay ahead.

That leads us full circle, doesn't it? They didn't know they were inspiring me. They weren't *trying* to inspire me. You can't make it an aim to be inspiring and short-cut the road to being an inspiring person. It would be very egotistical to make a virtue of yourself as being inspiring, yet you can definitely learn and practise the very habits that make a person one who inspires others. It seems that focusing on who I am becoming is the place to keep my attention, if I might ever hope to be inspiring to others. History will be the judge of whether we inspire anyone with our lives. We may get a little glimpse and be grateful, but it's never going to be something that Mandela would put on his CV.

If you have a moment, I'd love to know what you guys are reading currently. That reminds me of one book Jane and I have just finished by Richard Reed, one of the founders of Innocent Drinks, called *If I Could Tell You Just One Thing*,[56] in which he interviews lots of remarkable people, all of them inspiring in very different ways – people as diverse as Bill Clinton and Olivia Coleman, Jo Malone and Margaret Busby. When we'd finished the book, I asked Jane what she thinks makes people inspiring. Without missing a beat she said, 'They are all people who are gripped by something bigger than themselves – a purpose.' My hunch is that she is right. I hope I captured something of that in one of my previous letters.

Much love

Dad

STARTING A CONVERSATION

1. Who has had the greatest inspirational impact on your life so far and why?
2. What are you currently reading? What is interesting you? What are the ways in which you share what you are learning with others?
3. How does other people's inspiration lead to action in your life? What has inspired you and what action did it lead you to take?

9. Depth – go beyond the trivial

Hi guys

I have to tell you about dinner with Mike and Samantha Knowles last week. I'm sure you remember them from your childhood. We started in their lounge for drinks and snacks and chatted about the weather, the kids, their problems getting their internet fixed; all the usual stuff. Then we went into their cavernous farmhouse kitchen for the meal, which was delicious. What struck me was that the conversation didn't really move on from the pre-dinner small talk. The 'big' talk, the dinner table talk, was just another two hours of what I'd call chat. After an hour, I felt boredom, a little distraction and some frustration. I was thinking, 'Is this it? Is this as deep as we go? Four adults with a combined 200+ years of living and experiences and joys and struggles. Surely we can do better?'

So I tried asking questions to provoke some deeper thoughts on all the subjects we'd brushed over earlier in the lounge. What had they found most difficult, or rewarding, about parenthood? What were the underlying issues going on in their team at work? How were they balancing sustaining a relationship with two full-time jobs? I dropped in a few different things I'd been reading about potential and vocation and some of the underlying cultural shifts towards popularism. But no takers. I couldn't get a bite on any bait or hook that I threw out. I was left wondering whether I have difficulty staying on the surface level of conversations, whether I'm too intense or whether I'm judgmental about other people and what they do or don't talk about. I can talk football and weather like the best of them, but I do find it difficult to stay there.

I'm mindful of the wonderful line in *Thelma and Louise*, where one of the women is on the phone telling her husband she's leaving him and says, 'I guess we got what we settled for.' That's how it seems to me: we settle. Let me ask you, what do you want from your relationships with people? Is depth an issue that matters to you? At what point does surface become superficial, or the everyday become trivial? What do we want from each other? Can a relationship grow if it stays like a water boatman fly, on the surface of things? Is it about lack of content in conversations, or is it a lack of vulnerability? Do we only look for relationships that are as deep as we are ourselves? If I'm not struggling with the issues of my own life direction, meaning, motivation or darker side, maybe I don't look for people who are reflecting on these things themselves.

My hunch is that to grow in depth in our own lives, we need to have people around us who have depth in *their* lives – people who have gone deeper in themselves, who can help us to go deeper within us. Going deeper is like mining, because to become a deeper person takes intentionality, some hard work and struggle, some digging down.

In contrast to my dinner with the Knowleses are the words of renowned educationalist Paulo Freire, who said that humans are created to transform the world,[57] or Nelson Mandela's words about the purpose of life:

> What counts in life is not the mere fact that we have lived. It is what difference we have made to the lives of others, that will determine the significance of the life we lead.[58]

One of the reasons I'm drawn to Nelson Mandela is that he became a person of tremendous depth, shaped by his struggle around his passionate purpose for justice, which started early in his life. He was determined to make a difference from a young age and this drove him to read more, study more, seek to understand more and wrestle with his own demons in daily meditation. Every day in the rock quarry he would have risky, radical discussions with his fellow prisoners, where they ranged over every dimension of a re-imagined future for South Africa. He embraced feedback from his colleagues about his character, his strategies and his perspectives. These conversations were like the grit in the oyster shell, where struggle and agitation create the pearl.

I'm sure that becoming a person of depth must start with self-awareness. If I can't see myself, if I don't know myself, whether it's emotionally or in terms of attitudes, character, knowledge or health, then I won't seek more depth in any of these areas of my life. For Mandela, the pursuit of personal depth was the route he knew he needed to travel down if he was to achieve a purpose in life that was larger than himself, by making a difference in the lives of others. He refused to let go of his fight for justice and it had that deepening effect. When things don't change, *you* have to change. You have to become the change you want to see, as Gandhi once said. I don't imagine you'd ever get bored around the dinner table with him! However much time you had with Gandhi, or Mandela, there would always be more you wanted to dig into, explore and understand about those men.

There is a difference between being deep and being unnecessarily intense. Intensity is just being full of focused emotions, and is often as much about self-centredness, or ego, as about convictions. Intensity can make you blind to others rather than empathic. I've been asking people lately whether they think some people are deeper than others and generally they do, but interestingly the people who respond by saying 'I never really think about it' don't seem to have much to contribute about anything. Outwardly they appear accepting of life as it is, but also they don't seem to let life 'get' to them, prod them, poke them, dig deeper into them, to allow them to discover more of themselves. To me, being deeper is simply about becoming 'more' – more curious, more insightful, more self-aware, more passionate in my purpose in life.

Tell me, boys, am I just being judgmental and unaccepting? Those are the very ways I don't want people to behave to me. As a child it was always an insult for someone to call you 'a bit deep'. It inferred you should get out more, be playing football and 'having a laugh' with your mates. By adulthood, talking about certain things, like God or being 'spiritual', became synonymous with being ungrounded, not rational, somewhat flaky. It's like there's a suspicion of the deeper areas of life, wherever it's religion, psychology, philosophy, gender – anything that seems to go deeper than the everyday. Sometimes I feel like we have become a generation of simple soundbites.

Maybe it's a fear of what we don't know. I notice in Mandela and others that we regard as elders, not merely olders, is that they aren't one-dimensional. They have depth. When Mandela was on Robben Island, he would regularly attend the services of each religion when he could, because he was always a learner. He wanted to go deeper, further, become larger as a person. While his religious beliefs were private, he admitted to his close friend and fellow prisoner

Ahmed Kathrada 'I never gave up my Christian beliefs',[59] and his explanation of his hunger for depth was summed up in these words:

> I am not particularly religious or spiritual. Let us say I am interested in all attempts to discover the meaning and purpose of life. Religion is an important part of this exercise.[60]

In a letter to Winnie, he spoke of the necessity of daily meditation:

> The cell gives you the opportunity to look daily into your entire conduct, to overcome the bad and develop whatever is good in you. Regular meditation, say about fifteen minutes a day before you turn in, can be very fruitful in this regard.[61]

If you think you know the answers to everything, if you think you have arrived, if you think you have certainty, like 'there is no God', 'this is all there is', 'consciousness is just an issue of brain cells', then you stop asking questions, you stop wrestling with uncertainty and ambiguity. You stop learning.

We talk about 'growing up', but what we may ignore is the importance of 'growing down', like the roots of a tree. The moment you lose your curiosity for any area of life, it's like you put a lid on your own growth. The deepening process stops. The opposite is also true: if you keep questions central to your life, if you stay addicted to curiosity, then the adventure of going deeper, becoming larger, extending yourself further is always an open door.

One of the mantras I developed that has helped me most in recent years is 'there is more'. By that I mean that there is more of me – more levels of consciousness, more self-understanding, more depth of relationships, more growth of my mind, more inner healing, more I can do to improve my body, my diet, my lifestyle. I challenge myself to become *more* through my struggles, my questions, my interests, my motivations, my ideas. If you take the simple idea that life is a journey, then there's always farther to go, more to explore, more risks I could take, more skills I could practise, more or deeper relationships to develop. What one thing more could I do today than yesterday? Joseph Campbell's *The Hero's Journey* is a journey to discover more of myself, my resourcefulness, my creativity, my resilience, my meaning and purpose. Jung talks about that journey being in two stages, a first half of life and second half of life. This means that even though I have arrived at middle age, there is a whole lot more of me to discover in the second half.

Ken Wilber's writings on becoming a deeper person have helped me a lot over the past two decades, particularly his work on levels of consciousness.[62] Consciousness is such a fascinating area, because we all have it, but if you compare one person with another they seem to differ in the depth of that consciousness. You can prove that by simply asking a group of friends about some topical subjects, or how they define meaning, or what they're thinking about these days. The answers you will likely get range from 'Don't know, I haven't given it any thought' to 'That's interesting you ask, here's what going on for me right now and here are the questions I'm struggling with'. Some people are aware and awake at only a basic level. They are wondering what's for lunch and aware that they feel angry with their neighbour for cutting the lawn so early this morning. Others are aware of their intuitions about their relationships, what is going on in the culture at work; yet others are aware of a deep sense of presence that they would call Divine.

Wilber talks about the process of growing a deeper consciousness in terms of *waking up*.[63] This is where we begin to realise that there is more going on within us and around us in the world. We start becoming intrigued and curious about motivation, meaning and the dynamics of ourselves and our environment. The concept of waking up is why I decided to start meditating a few years ago. I knew I needed to wake up because my life wasn't working with me simply carrying on in a business-as-usual kind of way. I could tell there were frustrations and undercurrents within myself that I needed to start taking seriously.

Next, there is *growing up*. This is where we actually start investing in understanding more about our world and ourselves. We probably associate this with growing up emotionally, becoming more secure within ourselves, our psychological development. I used to use the psychometric test called the Myers Briggs Type Indicator,[64] which helps to identify personality preferences. I would run the test with teams and groups and once people had completed it you would see and hear 'aha' moments in the debriefing sessions, with people saying 'Wow, now I know why I do this' or 'That makes sense of my reactions to that particular situation'. Their self-awareness was beginning to grow. Similarly, going into a therapeutic conversation might help me to face up to a deep loneliness I had as a child, but found ways to cover over as I grew up. Now I have the chance to look at it and grow up a little more in an emotional sense.

The next level is what Wilber calls *cleaning up*. This is where we begin to own what is often called the shadow side of ourselves, where we realise that the feelings of anger we have towards someone else are actually our own problem with our self, not with them. It's easier to project my unexamined feelings onto someone else rather than admit that the problem is mine and do something about it. Apologising, learning to listen, changing unsustainable lifestyles – all of these are ways in which, because we are now more conscious, we start to clean up the mess we are leaving in the world, rather than blaming everyone else all of the time.

Finally, there is *showing up* – answering the call from the world to do something it needs us to do to change things for the better. Finding our purpose and engaging in the world with it. Bringing all of us into the world rather than hiding parts of us away, for fear of how others will react, fear of failure or vulnerability. Showing up means that we're awake, we're learning from life each day, cleaning up the negative things we dump along the path and meaningfully taking part in the world every day.

Another challenging perspective I got from reading Ken Wilber was to look at where my life is centred. Wherever the centre of my life is will shape the way I look at life. For example, if it is centred in me, *ego-centric*, then I am only going to look at the world as if I am the centre of everything: what *I* feel, what *I* want, what *I* believe, what *I* expect, what *I* need. While your little babies and toddlers are definitely at this stage of their development at the moment, you know there is more for them in the years ahead; they have a depth that lies beyond ego-centricity. If they don't discover that depth, then they will become unpleasant people to be around! In a normal maturing process, what we expect for your children's future is that they will move from being ego-centric to becoming *ethno-centric*. They will realise that they are part of a family, and of a larger group of people, a 'tribe'. They will become more conscious of being part of something larger than themselves. Again, this is fine when you are young and, in a sense, to cling loosely to as you grow older. But if you only root yourself in this stage, then you create a limited world of 'us' and 'them', in or out, my group or the opposition. The deeper level of awareness is called *global-centric*. We are all part of a highly interdependent world that is flooded with difference. The issues of our day are global, not national, and need global-centric leadership, people who make a virtue out of the differences and can see how they can work together to make a rich whole. Some would say there is an even deeper level, being *cosmo-centric*. Whether it's the depth psychology idea of someone like Jung, who said there is a collective (universal) unconscious, or the idea of a Divine or transcendent presence, cosmo-centricity locates our lives within a much larger story.

As Mandela reflected on the future and the challenges the twenty-first century would face, he said:

> We shall have to reach deep into the wells of our human faith as we approach the new century. No less than in any other period of history, religion will have a crucial role to play in guiding and inspiring humanity to meet the enormous challenges that we face.[65]

It is easy to write these things, but it's an enormous challenge to make the courageous shift from one level of consciousness to another.

In thinking about how one starts this journey of searching for greater depth in one's life, I'm encouraged by the fact that life itself gives us enough bumps and challenges to wake us up and give us the opportunity to get more curious.

If Abraham Joshua Heschel were here, he'd say to you both:

> There is meaning beyond absurdity. Know that every deed counts, that every word is power... above all, remember that you must build your life as if it were a work of art.[66]

Guys, if we're honest, life is absurd. You were nothing, then you were an embryo, then a baby with personality, then you grew and now you have little miracles of your own. You interact with this amazing world that is so complex, huge and miniscule at the same time, and yet it all seems to work, and you have the consciousness to be awed by it all – and then you die. If that isn't absurd, I don't know what is. Good guys lose, bad guys win, there seems to be little rhyme or reason as to who gets ahead or who gets caught under the heel of injustice. Yet beyond all of this is meaning. To go deeper as a person is to get curious and seek out that meaning. I think that's exactly what Mandela meant when he said 'I am interested in all attempts to discover the meaning and purpose of life'.

We can learn to start thinking through what we do, our daily actions. When Heschel says 'every deed counts', the question I can ask myself is: 'How did my deeds count today?' That was exactly what Mandela did each day in his meditation. When Heschel says 'every word has power', I can ask myself: 'How did I use my words today?' When he says 'build my life as if it were a work of art', my question would be 'What splash of paint did I put on my canvas today?' or, as Makoto Fujimura would ask, 'What did I make today?'

I have often wondered what it truly means to be intelligent, because I've seen many people who are academically very bright, but don't seem to have much wisdom regarding life and sometimes not much depth to them as people. The nearest I can get to a definition is that intelligence is simply the ability to think things through. We take so much at face value, or don't question it, or go by instinct or habit or what the media is shouting loudest about, but we don't take the time to think the issue through from A to Z for ourselves. Too often we leave others to do our thinking for us. It is this thinking-through, asking questions, being curious and staying with the uncertainties and not-knowings that creates our depth.

My last thought on this issue is that we need a safe space to grow. When I was a young child and my parents used to argue night after night, I would lay awake waiting for them to stop, wondering if one of them would leave and not be around when I woke in the morning. When you don't feel safe you hunker down, you make the world as safe as you can, and it affects how you think, or even if you think at all. It can become unsafe to explore 'more' in our lives. We know that extremes of conflict, anxiety and poverty actually reduce the brain's ability to think. We all need a safe space, but there is no growth without vulnerability. By writing or doing art or journaling or having good friends or places where we can be vulnerable and lay out within that safe space what we do know, what we do think, what consciousness we are aware of, we can begin to get curious, dig a little deeper, take a few small risks with ourselves and others and find more of ourselves as a result.

Years ago, I was meeting with a long-time friend from work. Over the years we had built up some solid trust. One day she started talking about God and faith, or rather not talking about it. What she said was she felt so conflicted by the whole subject of meaning in life that if such a conversation arose, she would just cry and get away from it. I asked her why. She had grown up and married into a mix of Muslim, Catholic, Hindu and atheist. Religion was a source of conflict in the home. She said she couldn't even get close to working out whose religion was true, because there was so much emotional turmoil within her whenever the issue was raised. I was hopefully empathic enough when I asked her, regardless of what her parents or anyone else believed, what she believed. What was hers? She said she didn't know; it was all a mess. I said, 'Tell me about the bits of the mess.' So she did. She didn't try to convince me, or herself, of anything. She just began to unpack years of feelings and thoughts and tears and questions and anger and slowly laid them out on the table, without any need to come to a conclusion. When I saw her a few months later, she told me how she had begun to find her own way through the maze of meaning and was trying to create a safe enough space for her daughter to do the same.

I'm feeling a little wary now. I'm fearful that I was a bit too deep in this letter, or maybe it's the fear of being too intense that I'm really worried about. Anyway, I hope we can talk about these thoughts.

Remember to bring the boys' bikes when you come next weekend. I have found a new path for them that I think they will love.

Much love

Dad

STARTING A CONVERSATION

1. Do you see yourself as a person of depth and why do you think so?
2. Who are the people around you that you see as people of depth and what is it about them that makes you say so?
3. Choose one area of your life and talk about how you might grow greater depth in that area.

10. Courage – have the value that makes everything happen

Hi guys

It's interesting to me that when I think about what I learned from founding the charity Emerging Leaders, I always end up returning to one key lesson: Just keep going. When you don't know what to do – just keep going. When you don't know how to get through the next funding crisis – just keep going. When you feel totally out of your depth – just keep going. The courage to keep going has probably – no, definitely – been the single most important thing I've done over the years. There were times when I remembered Winston Churchill's counsel, 'When you find yourself in hell, just keep on walking.' It was the rough reality of leadership, the times when I felt like I was in desperate places, that forced all the head knowledge I'd been carrying around with me into my heart and my awareness.

Another gem of wisdom from Churchill that I'd mentally filed away was that courage is the most important of all values, because every other virtue rests on it. Keeping going rests on courage. Keeping to your principles in life when you could take short cuts rests on courage. Making decisions that you believe to be right, but no one else understands, rests on courage. Speaking truth to power rests on courage. Courage is like the underlying muscle that makes all the other muscles work. You can have all kinds of ideals and values, but it is courage that makes us actually do something about them.

Courage was another of Mandela's clear virtues. Think of the countless times he was under threat, or arrested, or his family members were in danger, or he faced death at the hands of his enemies or illness in his body. You can see courage in his resolve to keep on moving forward in pursuit of justice, whatever the obstacles.

What I learned most from Mandela about courage is that it is grown, not inherited. We don't have a full tank of courage when we're born. Mandela believed that no one is born courageous, it is how we react to different situations that makes us so.[67] I'm sure we must all have some innate courage, but we have to fill the tank ourselves, we have to grow it. It's the fact that courage can be grown, and that an ordinary man like Mandela became exceptional because he took the time to grow it, that gives me the deepest hope that any of us can become our own version of Mandela, particularly in this domain. We can all develop courage like Mandela did. That was certainly his own conviction.

What will stop us growing courage is fear. On that point Mandela was very clear and most helpful:

> I learned that courage was not the absence of fear, but the triumph over it. I felt fear myself more times than I can remember, but I hid it behind a mask of boldness. The brave man is not he who does not feel afraid, but he who conquers that fear.[68]

How did Mandela conquer fear? He pretended to be brave. Yes, in his own words, when he was confronted by experiences where he was fearful (and there were many), he pretended that he was totally on top of the situation. For example, for his first imprisonment on Robben Island in May 1963, Mandela was herded towards his cell along with a bunch of other prisoners. As they were marched forwards the warders threaten them with death, and on arrival at the holding cell they were all made to strip naked. There was an incident in the line and a guard singled Mandela out for punishment. As the man approached to beat him, Mandela said, 'You dare touch me and I will take you to the highest court in the land and by the time I'm finished with you, you will be as poor as a church mouse.'[69] The guard stopped and didn't beat him. Mandela commented that he was very afraid, but he acted as if he was brave.

I don't know if I ever shared this story with you, but when I was nineteen years old, I took a summer job with a small construction company. I was trying to save some money for college and for travelling. One Friday afternoon the boss came to me and said there was an urgent 'rush' job the next day, if I wanted to earn some extra money – which I did! On Saturday morning I arrived early and worked hard all day and we got the job completed, which is always a very satisfying feeling. The boss was delighted and he handed over my cash payment for the day. As he put the money into my hands he said with a smile, 'Of course, this is a cash job – don't put this through your books; don't declare it to the Inland Revenue.'

I remember that awful feeling like a rabbit caught in the headlights, that twist in the gut. It was like an inner emotional traffic jam. Speak out and risk the response? Stay quiet and feel guilty? Guilty not just for the cheating, but also for the feeling within myself of not having the guts to honour my convictions. What should I do? Guys, you will have discovered for yourself by now that these moral moments, these 'doing the right thing' times, happen so fast that they catch you unawares and unprepared.

I drew in a deep breath and as he continued to turn away, I said, 'I always declare my earnings.'

There was a long, silent moment. He stopped in his tracks and slowly turned round. With some force, but sweetened with a reasonable tone and a continued smile, he replied, 'I know that normally that's the case, but this is a cash job and so it doesn't need to go through your books.' He turned away again, assuming that was the end of it. What should I do now?

I responded, 'I understand, but I always declare my earnings.'

The nice smile disappeared and the eyeballing began. 'Look, this is cash. We all get cash. If you declare this you risk getting everyone here into trouble if the auditors get onto it.' Now he was angry and his voice was climbing skywards, glazed with a veneer of threat.

I tried the only way out I could think of that both had integrity from my side and was respectful to him. I put the cash back into his hands. 'Look, you don't need to pay me for today. I'll do it for free. I've got no desire to get anyone into trouble, so you keep the money and the issue's resolved.' I started to walk away.

It didn't end there. He began shouting at me as I walked down the street, with people watching me being the focus of someone's anger. I felt so many emotions – strong, empowered, weak, confused, shamed, fearful – all at once. Mandela would have said, 'Of course you felt fear, that's normal, I would have too – but you made a choice to act bravely, to act courageously.'

I've been reflecting in my journal about courage and what I've learned from that day and many others since. Courage isn't easy. It takes courage to:

- Speak up.
- Hold your ground.
- Do the right thing and suffer the consequences.
- Live with so many conflicting emotions and yet keep on doing the right thing.
- Conduct a fearless moral inventory of yourself.
- Look your ego in the eye.
- Face up to your 'cracks' and fragility.
- Speak truth to power.
- Learn to think and act for yourself (but not selfishly) and not being co-dependent on others.
- Not give up.
- Get up after failure.
- Hang on until a crisis passes.
- Create something new.
- Apologise.
- Make the first phone call to a therapist.
- Go to see that therapist.
- Weed the garden of your own character each day.
- Do something for someone else.
- Fight for justice.
- Fight for human rights.
- Say 'no'.
- Break addictive behaviours and thoughts.
- Step out of your comfort zone.
- Keep going when you don't know what to do.
- Do the right thing even when it costs you your reputation, promotion, job or life.

Courage can be summed up in the words of Franklin Roosevelt:

> It is not the critic who counts; not the man who points out how the strong man stumbles, or where the doer of deeds could have done them better. The credit belongs to the man who is actually in the arena, whose face is marred by dust and sweat and blood; who strives valiantly; who errs, who comes short again and again, because there is no effort without error and shortcoming; but who does actually strive to do the deeds; who knows great enthusiasms, the great devotions; who spends himself in a worthy cause; who at the best knows in the end the triumph of high achievement, and who at the worst, if he fails, at least fails while daring greatly, so that his place shall never be with those cold and timid souls who neither know victory nor defeat.[70]

It has helped me to remind myself where the word courage comes from: *cor*, the Latin word for heart. Courage is about heart, not head alone. And we need different kinds of courage for life: moral courage, physical courage, mental courage, emotional courage, the courage to take risks, the courage to face down our demons, the courage to start up something, the courage to stop something, the courage to give feedback, the courage to receive feedback and the courage to step into the unknown. When you think about it, courage is something we probably need all the time.

I've been asking myself the interesting question of what I would do today if I had courage. What is not being done, left undone, not stopped, not spoken, where am I not summoning heart or courage? In terms of how we actually activate courage, that word 'summon' may be the key. It's like I need actually to call to myself – my head calling to my heart – 'Hey Trevor, keep going, speak up, take a risk here...' It's like calling to your legs to put one foot in front of the other.

Courage doesn't have any easy steps. Trying to have an honest conversation with my dad, the incident with the builder, wanting to give up when things got tough in a host of situations, facing up to myself, my own weaknesses and insecurities, all these took courage. The hardest steps of courage I've taken are the ones you know about and probably had the biggest impact on your lives. What steps of courage are being true to yourself and what are simply being selfish? Is it a step of strength or of weakness?

Richard Stengel lived and travelled with Mandela for years while helping him shape his autobiography, *Long Walk to Freedom*. Stengel sums up Mandela's view of courage this way:

> Mandela's highest praise for someone he considers courageous is 'he did very well'... that day in and day out, he resisted giving in to fear and anxiety.

He concludes, 'All of us are capable of that kind of bravery.' Those words, 'All of us are capable...', sum up the point of what these letters are trying to uncover. All of us are capable of becoming Mandela.

Even as I write to you both, I'm asking myself what I need courage for today. I'm thinking this is a good place to stop and pause for reflection.

I'll write again soon.

Love

Dad

STARTING A CONVERSATION

---

1. In which areas of your life do you most experience fear?
2. What would you do today if you had courage? What is not being done, left undone, not stopped, not spoken? Where are you not summoning heart and courage?
3. Who is the most courageous person you know and what could you most imitate about their courage?

---

11. Wisdom – metabolise your experience

Hi guys

I read these words from Allister Sparks in the *Guardian* a few years ago, about his first meeting with Nelson Mandela:

> My very first one-on-one meeting with him remains the most impressionable in my memory. For what I knew of him during those long years of incarceration was his reputation as the militant freedom fighter, the young Turk of the African National Congress's Youth League, who had played a key role in launching the resistance movement's first major defiance campaign in the 1950s, then gone on to lead its decision to turn to armed resistance and founded its armed wing, Umkhonto we Sizwe, the Spear of the Nation, in the 1960s.
>
> Yet the man I met at his Soweto home just two days after his release from the Victor Verster prison, near Cape Town, in February 1990, was a wise and thoughtful statesman, ready to negotiate peace and reconciliation with his people's oppressors and tormentors.[71]

A wise man. I think most people, if asked what they admired about the elder statesman Mandela, would reply that he was a wise man. What is wisdom and is it something we can develop, like the other characteristics of the man we've been discussing?

I like this quote from the *Washington Post*: 'Wisdom comes with age, except when it doesn't.'

When I was younger, I assumed that wisdom would come with age. You just got wiser as you got older. Now I know that isn't true. I've seen young people with 'wise shoulders' and I've met plenty of older people who don't seem to have graduated to a place of wisdom. I've concluded that people get wiser if they *work at* being wiser. Mandela worked at being wiser and it started when he was a child. He enrolled himself in the school of life. He signed up to be a learner. Being a learner is a precondition to wisdom. I don't just mean studying at school and passing exams, not that kind of learner, although of course that's important. I mean a learner of life. Mandela was curious from the start, as all children are. They only grow out of curiosity if adults don't feed their incessant questions or if they try to shut the children up. Mandela said of himself:

> Like all Xhosa children I acquired knowledge by asking questions to satisfy my curiosity as I grew up, learnt through experience, watched adults and tried to imitate what they did. In this process an important role is played by custom, ritual and taboos and I came to possess a fair amount of information in this regard.[72]

We know that in prison Mandela read and studied voraciously. He set up a university within the prison to encourage others to become learners as well. If I were to give a piece of fatherly advice to you, it would be to keep reading. Read deep, read wide, read who you agree with, read who you disagree with, listen to your own questions in any area of your life and read up about them. Podcasts are, of course, an amazing source of learning and I know you have both discovered that, for which I am delighted. Keeping on stretching yourselves through books, conversations, journaling, reflecting; this is the basic diet of wisdom.

But then you need to test out all you are learning in the classroom of life. I remember there being too little meaningful conversation around the dinner table when I was a child. The family table should be a place where we learn to speak out our ideas and have them challenged and shaped. The lack of this debate resulted in me lacking in confidence to offer a viewpoint on anything important as I got older. I was fearful of looking stupid. Saying nothing and doing nothing became a safe place. It's taken me years of hard work to step out of that and to put ideas and actions on the line.

The other key aspect that's key for developing wisdom, alongside being a curious learner, is the need for humility. A learner is just that... someone who is learning. So trying and failing are par for the course and they require humility: the honesty with oneself to know what you do and don't know and the willingness to be seen to get it wrong, in order to learn how to get it right.

Mandela never claimed anything other than that he'd made mistakes along the way, but what he did do was learn. The humility of wisdom means that we think before we speak, we don't assume we know the answers, we aren't obscured by our ego or power needs and we're honest about our mistakes and shortfalls.

The poet TS Eliot sums up the relationship between wisdom and humility perfectly in *The Four Quartets:*[73]

> Do not let me hear
> Of the wisdom of old men, but rather of their folly,
> ...
> The only wisdom we can hope to acquire
> Is the wisdom of humility: humility is endless.

We become wise; we aren't born wise. At its simplest level, wisdom is learning the art, rather than science, of knowing what to do, or what not to do, in any given situation. Wisdom isn't a rulebook, a manual of 'this is what you do in this situation', because every situation is different. Wisdom is a compass, not a map. Wisdom is where we develop the ability to make decisions on the best thing to do, or not to do, or how to do it. Wisdom is perspective gained through pain, experience, processing and time.

There is a saying in some of the ancient wisdom literature: 'Wisdom is proved by her children.'[74] I think that means that you can only judge a person's wisdom by their words and actions. For Mandela, wisdom was deciding to deal with PW Botha when no one else would. Wisdom was investing years in thinking through a future when they would be in power, even though they had been clearly told that they would die on Robben Island. Wisdom was the use of ubuntu,[75] an African leadership philosophy, to end Apartheid. Wisdom was wearing a Springboks shirt at the Rugby World Cup in 1995. Wisdom was limiting himself to a one-term presidency. Like everything else in becoming our version of Mandela, we can shout about it, big ourselves up, 'I am inspiring; I am wise; I am courageous', but that means nothing. It has to be true in our actions – and others will be the judge of that. For wisdom to be seen in the moment, in that instant decision or action, then it must have been developed a long time beforehand. You might say that wisdom is incubated until the right time, but it needs to be incubated so that it is *ready* for the right time.

The wisdom literature, as it's called, says we should pursue wisdom like our life depended on it, or pursue it like a lover or buried treasure. This is partly why I'm drawn to philosophy, *philo + sophia*, the love of wisdom. If we loved wisdom, we would not only have experiences - in fact we can't help having experiences, our day is made up of a continual flow of them - we would also ask ourselves what we learned from those experiences. Every experience is rich in wisdom, but we have to mine the experience to get the wisdom out of it. The wise person doesn't just 'do' life - they suck the juice out of it to get the lessons and the learning from it.

As I said earlier in this letter, reading is a great place for pursuers of wisdom. Reading the works of people who have thought deeply about many of life's rich and complex problems helps me to learn to think for myself. Reading good novels also helps me to think through how characters respond to the dilemmas of life.

Watching the wise at work is yet another way of pursuing wisdom. Mandela talked about watching his elders and learning from their actions. It is interesting how Stengel[76] shaped his book about the experience of years following Mandela around: he made each chapter a window into the man's wisdom. How to develop courage, how to lead from the front and from the back, how to be principle centred, how to know your enemy and how to work with your rivals. How to play the long game in life and how to know when to say yes and when to say no. He even examined Mandela's wisdom on the subject of when it is wise to quit.

I have a question for you; a few, actually. Do you watch certain people (elders) in your life and learn from them? Can I ask who you learn from? Is it too soon to ask if you aspire to be an elder to others when you get older, and whether you are investing in that now, incubating your wisdom through your curiosity and learning? Do you journal, reflecting on and processing your daily experiences to turn them into wisdom?

Big questions, I know. But we can talk more when we meet soon.

Much love

Dad

STARTING A CONVERSATION

1. Who do you see as wise and what do you observe about them?
2. Choose one recent experience in your life and take a deep dive into all the aspects of wisdom that it could give you. When you think you've discovered everything, ask yourself: 'And what else?'
3. Take one decision you need to make, choose three people you know (alive or dead) - one of who could be Mandela - and ask yourself: 'What would this person decide in this situation and why?'

12. Vision – create tangible hope

Hi guys

When I think back to the conception of Emerging Leaders, I have a feeling that it almost started itself: it propelled itself into existence. You'll remember that in 2005 I was in Zambia, visiting a school I'd helped to get started, and the trip overwhelmed me with the immensity of the challenges of extreme poverty. At every level of community life people were suffering, and I wasn't prepared for the devastating impact it all had on me. Nothing in the community seemed to be working. I couldn't walk away from what I was seeing, but equally I had no idea what I could do to help. I had never before felt so impassioned and powerless at the same time. How could I possibly get the kind of leadership development that was needed to help people help themselves out of poverty?

It reminds me also of when I completed writing and publishing *The 18 Challenges of Leadership*, thinking to myself: What next? I think I even discussed it with you both at the time. What I actually said to myself was, 'What would a good leader do now?'

The simplest definition of leadership I ever came up with was 'leaders are people who lift up their head'. Non-leaders are busy walking with their heads facing downwards, looking at what's in front of their nose, what's in their inbox, who's chasing them on the phone, what the terrain looks like right now and how to organise and navigate themselves through it. By contrast, leaders lift up their head so that they can see the future and walk towards it. Their feet are firmly on the ground (they are realists) and their eyes are on the horizon (they are visionaries).

I had a wake-up call on this issue of vision again recently. I had always thought I was a man of vision, but I have to be honest, for the first time this past weekend I found myself thinking that right now, I feel like I lack vision. I've found myself getting so wound up, and at times quite depressed, by all that's going on in our country. In all my decades I've never felt like we are so adrift, in so many ways. As you know, I've been thinking a lot recently about courage and wisdom - where do I need to exercise courage to speak up or take action? What does wisdom dictate? What's the best thing to do, or not do? How can I do it? What I came face to face with over the weekend is that I lack any real sense of what I hope the future will actually look like. I don't have a vision of the future when it comes to my role in society right now. I'm unhappy with the present, but that isn't vision. In my experience, real vision brings hope: the feeling that things will be better in a new, re-imagined future, which is how it will look when things have changed. Someone once said of vision that you need to be able to see yourself in the future, like seeing yourself as an actor in a film. Can I see myself in a particular version of what the future could look like?

What Mandela had, what Martin Luther King had, was a dream:

> Ours is a vision of a just and democratic South Africa in which all its people will enjoy a full and rewarding life.[77]

Both of these men could see, in their mind's eye, what justice and racial integration would look like. They could see mixed ethnicities sitting at the same café table, going into the same public toilets, sitting next to each other on the buses. Vision and hope sit alongside each other as inseparable twins. Vision and hope are what give you the energy, the fresh breath, to get out of bed and put your efforts into making that future a reality.

Facing up to my lack of vision seemed to be the catalyst for me to actually create a vision. It gently forced me to ask myself what the future is that I want to see. I started making notes on the whiteboard in my study and as the hours progressed, I could see a shape emerging for the future I desire. I could see myself mentoring young social entrepreneurs around the world and encouraging them to aspire to become the next Mandelas for their own generation.

Having a vision is what gave Mandela both a compass and the stamina to keep going:

> Part of being optimistic is keeping one's head pointed towards the sun, one's feet moving forwards. There were many dark moments when my faith in humanity was sorely tested, but I would not and could not give myself up to despair.[78]

Vision is like a compass. When we are making a journey and lack a map, because no one has ever been down that particular road before, then we need a compass. It gives us a direction to travel when the roads are unclear or don't exist yet. Mandela put this idea about a compass in his own words when he was presented with the Chris Hani Award for Peace:

> This is a lesson for all of us to live our lives by: that the ways in which we will achieve our goals are bound by context, changing with circumstances

> even while remaining steadfast in our commitment to our vision.[79]

The context, the circumstances, are often changing. They move around like the swirling sea. I see this every day in my work. You think a person you hired will stay for years and they're gone in months; you think an opportunity will open great doors and the key person doesn't reply to your emails. You'll see it with your own kids – you think they will do one thing and they'll head off in a totally different direction. Context and circumstances truly are always changing. But a vision in life gives us a story to head towards, regardless of the messiness and challenges of today. It is our commitment to the vision, rather than the current circumstances, that gives us the courage and the hope and the energy to keep on moving forwards.

However, small bear traps do linger for leaders in this word 'vision'. Of course, in one sense 'vision' is the right word, because it's all about seeing and that is what vision means. But it's a bear trap because, just as walking with your head down can lead you to become a function of the present situation, so also just lifting your head up can result in looking up and accepting what lies on the horizon. True vision for leaders has three dimensions, each prefixed by one essential word: *create*. Leaders don't just inhabit a laid-out future, they create it. They see what their eyes show to them and then they re-imagine it. They ask themselves, 'What *could* this look like?'

The first dimension of vision is to *create perspective*. Perspective challenges us to challenge ourselves about what we are seeing in front of us. One of my favourite writers, Ken Wilber, has an integral approach that teaches us to look at every issue from at least four perspectives. There is a personal, subjective viewpoint (what it looks like from inside my own mind, emotions, attitudes); there is a personal, objective viewpoint (what it looks like from an external observer's point of view); but then there are also two collective perspectives. The first is sometimes called a paradigm, how we together see this situation from the inside of our group, tribe or organisational culture, what it feels like to us. The second is how the situation is observed from the external perspective, asking what an observable fact would be if a group of people were looking at the same issue.

Spiral dynamics is another perspective builder. We talked about this at Christmas. The image I use is of climbing a spiral staircase. At ground level there is only antagonism or negotiation. Spiral dynamics encourages us to climb upwards and see the issues from higher and higher perspectives. The personal can be seen from the level of the tribe, group or family; the tribe can be viewed from the level of the globe; the globe can be viewed from the level of the universe; and the universe can be viewed from the level of the transpersonal. With each shift upwards in perspective, new understanding and new solutions are revealed. Vision is created through perspective.

Once I heard the true story of two lovers being torn apart by family pressures because of two totally different cultural and faith backgrounds. The perspectives of these warring attitudes were getting inside the couple's relationship. A wise person counselled them both to choose the book that was dearest to their heart, one that captured their faith and culture and heart, a book that they would dearly love their partner to read. They swapped precious books and as they read the book they had been gifted, each found a deep insight into their partner's worldview, their heart, their faith, their culture and their love perspectives. When they met and shared all they had learned, they discovered that their learning had created a whole new space between them that transcended the polarised views they were being pressured with. It was no longer a conflict, it was no longer his view/her view, it wasn't a negotiation with winners and losers, it was a new way of seeing the world, each other and a life together, within this larger perspective.

Perspective is so important in life. Desmond Tutu and the Dalai Lama speak of its primary importance in the *Book of Joy*.[80] We talk about 'getting things out of perspective', by which we generally mean that we've let things get bigger in our minds than they should be and assume more importance than they need to have. Perspective allows us to get up very close to what we are doing or feeling right now, and then it allows us to step back and take a look from a distance, in order to see how what we are doing right now fits into the bigger picture of life. Perspective makes sure that all of the little 'close-up' steps we take in life actually fit together in the larger life story that we want to write.

Jane has taught me that artists have to learn about this. The golden rule from the masters is that you step in close to your painting and put on a brush stroke or two, and then you step back to get some perspective. Step in, step out, step in, step out. You can use your instincts when you are up close, but that doesn't give you perspective. Vision lies in the stepping out, in checking that what we are doing right now is getting us to where we are trying to go. Vision allows us to check each stroke against the larger picture we are seeking to paint. Vision allows us to ask: 'Does this action get us closer to our vision, add to our vision, or does it detract from our vision?' It's this that makes vision such a practical necessity in life. It's the key to making judgements and decisions every day.

The second dimension of vision is to *create the future*. Leaders don't just see what is, what can be viewed with the regular eye, they see how they want it to be: 'How do I want the future to look? How do I want to be as a person in the future?' You gave me a book once called *Re-imagining Rwanda*,[81] and that word 're-imagining' has stuck with me ever since. When you look into the future you can imagine how it will be, but, more than that, how you *want* it to be. You can re-imagine how you desire it to be.

When I first visited the Dandora area of Nairobi, Kenya, back in May 2012, it was one of the poorest, most dangerous, most unhygienic places in the city, especially as it was built on a vast garbage dump. If you drew a straight line from then to the future, you could see what Dandora would look like in ten or twenty years from now. But that isn't vision, it's just sight. It isn't re-imagining the future. What the young people who were beginning to own their own leadership potential asked themselves was, 'What kind of future would amaze us here? What could Dandora become positively famous for?' Music and dance and art were emerging as a vibrant force among the local youth and so they re-imagined Dandora by saying, 'What if Dandora were to become famous as a centre for excellence for youth in the area of the arts? What if, when you thought of brilliant hip hop, the first word that would come to your mind would be... Dandora?' And because they re-imagined the future, this then-impossible future became a vibrant reality – it's now called Hip Hop City!

The young leaders of Dandora embodied the leadership of vision summed up in the words of poet and philosopher John O'Donohue:

> May you have a mind that loves frontiers so that you can evoke the bright fields that lie beyond the view of the regular eye.[82]

Hip Hop City is a bright field that is bringing hope to youth across Nairobi.

I've come to see that the third dimension of vision is to *create a legacy*. Like the knight Parsival in the legends of King Arthur, we must learn to ask the fundamental question as we search for the holy grail of leadership: 'Who does the Grail serve?' Vision for whom? Vision in the service of what?

Mandela's close ally, Cyril Ramaphosa, said of him:

> He's a historical man, he was thinking ahead of us. He had posterity in mind. How will they view what we've done? And history has absolved him. It turned out exactly as he thought it would.[83]

This is the vision of legacy. What is the story we want to write *beyond* this horizon, not *on* the horizon? Many leaders can get as far as the horizon, but only the wisest of leaders goes beyond – beyond the horizon of their tenure, or their career, or their lifetime. True leadership looks beyond.

You know Eddie? Of course you do. Well, his dad once said to him, 'Eddie, the most unselfish thing you can do is to plant a walnut tree, because you probably won't see the fruit in your own lifetime.' As any of us create families, organisations or even nations, it would be good to ask ourselves how the future will judge us. In our case, what investment will you see that I made in the past, so that you will be able to reap the story you enjoy in the future – a future that is sustainable, just, peaceful and equal? As Stengel concluded of Mandela, 'He was looking over the horizon', always seeing the point you cannot glimpse with the naked eye, in order to create a legacy for future generations that cannot yet be perceived.

What I want to leave with you is the idea that when leaders are said to be people of vision, it means they are creating all three of these dimensions:

- The vision of perspective.
- The vision of re-imagining.
- The vision of legacy.

The challenge to all of us remains: having a vision for our life is an act of leadership. It happens because we are intentional; it happens because, like all good leaders, we don't work at 100% capacity. We work with space, with free thinking time that allows us to climb up to the highest vantage point, look around and into the future, and re-imagine what we want to be happening in our work, or relationships, or world in that future. Some people think that creating vision is 'fluffy' or idealistic, but such a vision is really quite grounded. Asking myself what I will be doing in my re-imagined future makes it intensely practical. What do you think Mandela and his team were endlessly discussing in the rock quarries of Robben Island? They were discussing their vision of the future, which for them meant how exactly their country would operate if it was truly a rainbow nation; how education or housing would work; how they would deal with truth and reconciliation.

One of Mandela's key lessons to us is that without vision, we lose our way.

How do you see your futures? I'd love to know.

With love

Dad

STARTING A CONVERSATION

1. Think of a time when you felt you had a vision. How did it shape what you did, how you felt and what you achieved?
2. Who is the best visionary you know? What habits can you learn from them?
3. If you were to create a vision for a legacy in one area of your life, describe in as much detail as possible what the future would look like.

13. Resilience – develop more than 'bounce-back'

Hi guys

I remember the joy of going to children's parties when I was young and discovering these almost life-sized blow-up cartoon characters, like Mr Blobby or Yogi Bear. This large toy would be in the middle of the room and the game was to punch it hard and watch it bounce right back to a standing position. The thing about these toys was that however hard you hit them, they did in fact bounce back, totally upright. Every time. You could try to outwit them by hitting them from one angle and then another, but the result was the same – they bounced back. They had this perpetual bounce-back because of ballast, water or sand poured in through an opening at the base of the toy. The ballast was the weight that ensured there was more weight in the toy's centre of gravity than the strength of the punches landed on it. One word we often use for 'bounce-back' is resilience, of which Mandela was a clear example. How many times did he receive a knock-out punch from his enemies or from circumstances and not just get up, but seem to become stronger?

Why do we need resilience? Because life is tough. For some people it is tough some of the time and for many people in the world it is tough all the time. There are so many ways to get knocked down. We defeat ourselves with our attitudes, or we get caught under the wheels of other people's expectations or criticisms. Then there are life's challenges, like COVID-19, or poverty, sickness or redundancy. How we keep going and keep growing through these punches is at the heart of resilience.

What underlies resilience to give us a foundation for bouncing back? Courage is certainly one thing, as I've written to you about before. Self-esteem is another form of human ballast that is at the foundation of our ability to struggle on, regardless of what life throws at us. Building our self-esteem and that of our children is vital to the capacity to be resilient by developing a basic self-belief, an attitude that says: 'I may not know what to do, but I will find a way through this difficulty.' The wonderful poem by Maya Angelou, 'I Will Rise', is her testament to this self-belief, or what she calls a nobleness of spirit, where she describes the racial, sexual and circumstantial knocks she received in her life. But at each point of knock-down her response was the same – *I will rise.*

My brother always had the philosophy of life that what doesn't kill you will make you stronger, although I don't know how much he heeded it. Archbishop Desmond Tutu described how prison was a time of deep growth for Mandela, where he discovered how adversity could make him stronger, even in lifetime imprisonment. Tutu said:

> I think what happened to him in prison was something that you have to now accept my authority for it, that suffering can do one of two things to a person. It can make you bitter and hard and really resentful of things. Or as it seems to do with very many people—it is like fires of adversity that toughen someone. They make you strong but paradoxically also they make you compassionate,

> and gentle. I think that that is what happened to him.[84]

Somehow Mandela made friends with his suffering. It became his way of growing to be a bigger person in his character and in wisdom. How does that work? When tough things happen to us, they pose a deep question about who we are:

- Are you up to this?
- Are you any good at this?
- Do you matter?
- Does anyone care about you?
- Are you worth anything?

They also expose our vulnerabilities and give us the opportunity to work on them.

I remember the night before my birthday, almost two years ago exactly to the day. Having gone through the low moment of my second cancer diagnosis in six years, I was assuming it would now be an uphill but winnable fight back to full health. But that October evening the consultant said the post-treatment numbers weren't going down as fast as he'd expected. You could see it on his face and then in his explanations of why the numbers might not be as good as he'd hoped. Of course, he started with simple explanations like infections, but explanation number five (I remember it clearly) he called the 'doomsday scenario'. This is where the cancerous cells have gone AWOL in your body and no one knows where they are. In that moment you feel yourself falling down a deep hole and you wonder how you'll be able to climb back out. That was the hard punch. Resilience was going to be about what happened within me the next morning, how I responded to my fears. (As it turned out, it wasn't option five, thankfully.)

Suffering is such a relative term, isn't it? Some people would say I've suffered as I've had cancer twice, but it doesn't feel that way. Don't get me wrong, it's no barrel of laughs getting the diagnosis and undergoing the treatments, but compared to others I have seen I got away very lightly, both times. We too easily use the word 'suffering', but I think we need to be a bit more precise and ask 'suffering what?' What I have learned about tough times – illness, relationship breakdowns, work meltdowns – is that they all cause pain in a different way. Suffering is about how we experience our pain in the various shapes in which it comes, whereas resilience is about how we deal with that pain when it arrives. To be honest, I had more physical suffering when my back muscle went into spasm than with either cancer. But cancer wakes us up to a different kind of pain: emotional pain. Fears of death, fears of loss, feelings of abandonment and loneliness, anguish and anxiety. So our perception of the pain is as real as the actual pain itself.

Mandela suffered physical pain and hardship, whether by mistreatment from his captors or the back-breaking work in the quarries on Robben Island. But his deeper pains were when his mother died, or his children died and he wasn't allowed out of prison to go to their funerals, or separation from his wife and hearing how she was being brutally abused. Most people seem to speak of his suffering in prison for twenty-seven years as one thing, but in reality it was many things, many different responses to many different kinds of pain. And it didn't start or end with Robben Island. The aspect I want to talk about in this letter is the fact that he kept going. The pain didn't ultimately define him or defeat him, although there were times when it easily could have done, especially if he hadn't had his friends around him in prison.

The question I wrestle with is: 'How do you keep going through the pains of life?" And more than that, how can the pain shape who you are becoming? Some people call this resilience, some endurance, others bounce-back. Statistician and essayist Nassim Taleb takes this even further and calls it being antifragile.[85] What he means is that the opposite of fragile isn't just resilience or bounce-back, returning to how things were, it's actually using the pain to create something better and stronger than before. How can I grow, become a bigger person, through this experience, not just survive it?

If I could say anything to you guys as you grow up, it's that you should prepare yourself for pain. It will come. It's already come to you both in relationships and tough birth experiences, as well as the struggles of your close friends. I remember years ago when you were both very young and I'd taken you to one of these warehouses converted into massive play centres. We'd gone with your grandma Daisy. You were old enough to occupy yourself for hours on the wonderful range of apparatus, on which parents (and grandparents) weren't allowed, so I sat with the book called *Grace and Grit*, by Ken Wilber.[86] It was about the death of his wife and how they dealt with her dying. Such a moving and insightful book. Grandma leant over at one point and asked me what I was reading. So I told her. You could see her mind working as she looked at you two young kids, full of energy, and then looked at me and the book. 'That's a bit of a macabre thing to be reading, isn't it?' she asked.

I had decided to read it to prepare me for the future. I had decided to read it when I didn't need it, so I would be prepared for when I did need it. I knew a time was coming when I would have to face the death of my parents and others close to me, and I knew that I needed to prepare myself by thinking through someone else's experience.

In prison, Mandela read the classic Greek plays. Why did he do that? To inspire and prepare and strengthen himself to get through his own suffering. He said:

> What I took out of them was that character was measured by facing up to difficult situations and that a hero was a man who would not break even under the most trying circumstances.[87]

He fed himself with the experiences of others to help him to manage his own experiences. Getting prepared for pain goes a long way, because you've already created some response pathways in your brain; you've laid some mental tracks for your thoughts to go down when the crunch comes.

Pain is a gift that no one wants. I say a gift, because it does something in you that nothing else can, but it's... well, painful. And who wants that? I see pain as like surgery itself. It digs deep into us and exposes the truth about us to ourselves. Pain showed me how fearful I was of death; it showed me how much I resist having to look at my own ego and insecurity issues; it showed me how addicted I am to staying in control of myself; it showed me deep feelings of loneliness and abandonment that had always been there but I had protected myself against. It showed me that there was more depth to me to be explored than I had imagined. Pain breaks through to deeper levels of consciousness; levels that I had read about, but didn't know I had.

What I discovered through pain is that there are many little deaths, not just the big final one. Being mortal, being human, has many meanings. If death is the absence of life, then a threat to any place with which I associate myself, my identity, who I am and anything I feel gives me life will seem like a death. Pain is a blunt instrument to kick the scab off all my unhealed ego wounds.

For example, I have a deep fear of abandonment. It goes back a long way and I never really seem to get to the bottom of it. What pain does is makes me afraid I'm going to die and that will be the ultimate experience of abandonment. Your lives, Jane's life, everything will go on without me and from my perspective that will feel like abandonment (I know it isn't very rational, but then none of this stuff is). So the pain beneath the pain of any sickness is actually a deeper psychological pain: abandonment. You will probably discover your own pathology in time. Seen in this light, pain actually does me a favour: it wakes me up to deeper parts of myself that I avoid, but when I allow the pain to help me face these unknown places, it can deliver a level of healing and develop a level of consciousness that otherwise wouldn't be there.

There is something freeing when you let pain do its work. What I mean is that there are so many things we hold on to that keep us stuck where we are, rather than freeing us up to become more than we currently are. I hold on to my need to feel good about myself, safe, secure, admired, in control, successful. If my fingers grip tightly to all of these things, then what pain does is prise my fingers off all I hold dear. Once you've faced the worst, once your fingers are off the controls and you realise that actually you're still alive, life hasn't collapsed, you're still breathing, you're fundamentally OK, then you are free to make different choices. What kind of choices? One example is the choice to make the most of your life.

Victoria Derbyshire is a prime-time TV presenter who had extensive treatment for breast cancer. It is now over three years since her treatment and her response to the choices she now has is summed up in these words: 'Pre-cancer, I lived life to the full – now I feel like it's off the scale.'[88] She could have chosen despair and hopelessness, but she chose to become a larger person. The same is true of all those close associates imprisoned with Mandela. Incarceration and injustice against them could have made them smaller people, not greater. But they made different choices. They embraced life, they carried on being learners, activists and... elders. They carried on becoming, growing, because they knew that every day was a gift. Playing a safe game of life limits any of us from fulfilling our potential.

Another of the freedoms that come from letting pain deliver its gifts is in our character. We've often discussed this issue and it's a humbling one for me. You know me as your dad, but you also know me for my character, and my character is what dominates what you think of me and how you relate to me. It's not my role title of 'dad', or 'CEO' or whatever that walks through the door to greet you. The first thing that registers in your head and heart is my character and there is no hiding from that. All trust relies on good character and trust is everything in all aspects of life (even economist Tim Harford says that 99.5% of the economy is based on trust[89]). This is also true for Mandela. When we think about who he became, we think as much about his character as anything else. And his character was directly shaped by his suffering. In his own words:

> The policy of apartheid created a deep and lasting wound in my country and my people. All of us will spend many years, if not generations, recovering from that profound hurt. But the decades of oppression

> and brutality had another, unintended effect, and that was that it produced the Oliver Tambos, the Walter Sisulus, the Chief Luthulis, the Yusuf Dadoos, the Bram Fischers, the Robert Sobukwes of our time–men of such extraordinary courage, wisdom, and generosity that their like may never be known again. Perhaps it requires such depth of oppression to create such heights of character.[90]

The pain is like the refiner's fire: it exposes what is in my heart, what is in my attitude, and once that is exposed then I have a choice, an opportunity, to become someone different. Just as the 'fire' reveals my pride, then I now have the opportunity to start practising humility. Character is simply the result of those years of unchallenged thoughts becoming attitudes and actions. Pain gave me another chance with myself. The Greeks had a process called docimacy, where you put base metal into a pot over a fire and turn up the heat. The intense temperature forces the dross to the surface of the pot, where it is seen and can be removed to effect cleansing. Then the temperature is turned up again, more impurities are revealed on the surface and there is more opportunity to clean up the dross. Pain has this effect if we let it. But I also know that I fight the opportunity to change as much as I embrace it. Developing character is a lifetime's work.

The toughest lesson for me with pain has been to lean in to it. I don't mean to sadistically revel in it, but rather to lean into the gifts it may give you. My observation is that people who face death before they die free themselves up to live life to the full now. When Mandela prepared to give his final defence in the Rivonia trial, he knew he was likely to be sentenced to death. It was the sentence everyone expected. His speech to the judges reflected a man for whom looking his own death in the eye had freed him up to speak truth to power in the courtroom, knowing that it might be his final chance to say anything meaningful to the watching world:

> During my lifetime I have dedicated myself to this struggle of the African people. I have fought against white domination, and I have fought against black domination. I have cherished the ideal of a democratic and free society in which all persons live together in harmony and with equal opportunities. It is an ideal which I hope to live for and to achieve. But if needs be, it is an ideal for which I am prepared to die.[91]

Or consider the Dalai Lama, whose painful lifetime exile from his Tibetan homeland and people has been so hard. How does he deal with this? He practises a death meditation regularly, to free himself to face the actual day of his death without fear.

The Bible talks about losing your life (while you are still alive) in order to find it. Catholic martyr Charles de Foucauld had a daily prayer of surrender. I heard the novelist and essayist Pico Iyer speak on the radio recently and he had the same message: by the age of thirty or forty the reality of our mortality starts us asking the big questions of life. Iyer stresses that we should do this work now. He says that all of the world's major religions use a form of meditation, which in itself is a way of practising dying before dying, a way of letting go, surrendering to something bigger or deeper beyond yourself.

I think I said to you before that if I have one regret it's that I came late to meditation and it was pain that brought me there. When I was working in South Africa a few years ago, the work was tough and I could feel it affecting my health. This went on day after day and I was getting more and more worked up within myself. A thought went through my head that I wasn't going to survive if I continued working like this. It was a clear and transforming moment. It was as if I said to myself that if I don't learn to meditate, I'll die. I know that sounds very dramatic, but it was. Pain drove me to meditate and meditation allowed me to begin the process of facing down the mortality behind my pain.

So there is much about pain that is totally undesirable and yet it has many gifts too. It gives us hope, character, freedom, a shift from *doing* to *being*, facing questions of meaning and purpose, opening up deeper levels of consciousness, exposing our ego, keeping us human and humble, and it sorts out what is essential from the novelties of life. For me, becoming resilient, or antifragile, is developing this richer pool of resources, the ballast in the toy, to draw from, to keep on moving forwards when the going gets tough, like it did that time with the doctor's bad news a few years ago.

Enough for now. Maybe we can explore these thoughts a little if we have some time together after your auntie's party in a fortnight's time.

Much love

Dad

STARTING A CONVERSATION

1. Think through recent challenging situations where:
   (a) you felt you 'bounced back' well.
   (b) you felt you grew through the experience.
   (c) you feel you continue to get defeated.
2. What does pain mostly reveal to you about yourself and how could you use this insight to grow?
3. Think about three people you would count as 'resilient'. What is it that they do to make them like that?

14. Leadership – write your own life story for the benefit of others

Hi guys

I remember one very hot evening in Stellenbosch, South Africa. I had been asked by one of our funding partners to meet the boss of one of the largest auditing companies of global supply chains. People were spilling across the town's central streets in search of the best place for sundowners and I was seeking the small restaurant where dinner had been booked. It took some hunting down, as the restaurant's façade was narrow and the crowds were obscuring everything. When we were finally seated at our table and the introductions had been made, our guest went straight to the point, to the surprise of both my host and me: 'I've heard about your work. Very impressive, but where I struggle is that you can't honestly believe that everyone is a leader, do you? I mean, that would create all kinds of trouble and anarchy in the workplace, wouldn't it?'

That 'wouldn't it?' was said with a force that was meant to elicit agreement from me in reply. Our partner hadn't told me how sceptical this man was about what we were doing. I hoped I wasn't about to upset anyone, but hopefully I was kind and firm in my response: 'Yes, I am convinced that everyone on the planet has the potential to be a leader at some level – personal and relational at the very least.'

The guest came straight back: 'That cannot be and it would be dangerous to let people think so. There would be chaos. There would be too many bosses and, as I said, there would be anarchy from people when they realised they had been "bigged up" only to be let down when they discovered they weren't going to be promoted.'

I responded, 'I think there's a confusion here. It sounds like you are talking about people in positions of leadership, roles of leadership, people with the title of leadership on their office door. Of course not everyone has the *position* of leadership, but that doesn't mean that everyone hasn't got the potential and the ability to be the leader of their own life.'

The conversation continued for the next few hours, before we all graciously parted ways into the now quietening streets. The debate that evening about whether leadership is for the few or for everyone was typical of many other conversations I've had over the years and for me embodies a fundamental question about human potential.

I can remember even in late primary school being aware of the idea of leadership. I saw simply that the offer was there for anyone to get on and get something done, make something happen, get off the benches and get onto the pitch of life. That's why a few of us started a school Save the Children club, in response to the Biafra famine that we were hearing about. That straightforward child's view was reinforced over my teenage years and wonderfully enlarged in my late teens and early twenties by my personal exposure to some outstanding leaders in both the UK and Europe – people who through the weight of their character or their actions made something happen that was benefiting the world. What I can also remember is standing in a desperately poor Zambian suburb and realising that everyone is and needs to be the leader of their own life if they are to haul themselves out of poverty. The basic leadership skills and character that are required of a great organisational leader are also needed by every individual – it's just the context and the complexities that are different.

I recently heard a rabbi speak to 2000 young people at a conference in London, where he mentioned a great saying: 'Before I say a word, I am its leader; after I say a word, I am its slave.'[92] What it says to me is that while the thought remains inside my head, I can lead it, direct it, shape it, for the good of others. Once I've spoken it out loud, I no longer have control over its impact, so I need to lead my thoughts and words carefully before they leave my mouth. Along with our thoughts and words, we can also lead our actions, our choices and the shape of our relationships. We can lead our own livelihoods, health and learning too.

One morning when you were still at primary school, I was sitting in the library of Southampton University. I used to go and work there when I needed some quiet. I wasn't a student there, so I would sneak inside to find a quiet desk hidden amid the ocean of books. When I got weary of what I was doing or I needed inspiration, I would get up and browse the shelves. In the business section I happened to pick up Howard Gardner's book *Leading Minds*,[93] and it was in that book that I found the key I had been looking for. Gardner, a Harvard professor, had made a study of numerous leaders across the world to try to understand how leaders think and what their mindsets were. Was there a common idea of what leadership is and how a leader's mind works? This is the definition he distilled from his research:

> Leadership is the ability to create a story that affects the thoughts, feelings and actions of others.

There it was – the word 'story'. Of course, he wasn't talking about *The Cat in the Hat* or the latest Harry Potter, he was talking about real stories, stories from life. Every single human on the planet has a real story, every relationship has a story and every business has a story. Every one of us is involved in writing a true-life story every day, whoever we are, whatever we do. *You* have a story. You are living it right now. One day you were born and each day since you have shaped the true story you are still writing today. Although you both share the same parents and you come from the heritage of all your grandparents' stories, you are both writing a unique story of your own. Both of your stories aren't the same, but each influences the other. Gardner says that our stories 'affect the thoughts, feelings and actions of others', in good ways or not so good, leaving the world a better place than we found it or a worse place. I discovered that there are over 400 definitions of leadership, but they all have one thing at their heart – influence, impact on others. Our lives are either part of the problems in the world, or they are part of the solutions.

Authority, a word we often associate with leadership, has embedded within it the word *author*. An author has power over the story: they create it, shape it, decide where it goes and where it doesn't go. The author has the pen. But here's the rub. While all of us have the potential to have authorship (author-ity), to lead our own lives, we don't all do it – we give away our pen, or someone takes it from us.

I remember coaching someone from the head office of one of the High Street banks. When I met him my first impression was of a man who was older than his years, with a tiredness you see in some people when it seems the life has been drained out of them. As I got to know him and built up some trust, I found myself reflecting to him that I couldn't help notice he seemed very unhappy. It was a bit of a risky thing to say, but it was so obvious. He opened up and told me how much he hated his job, always had, how he couldn't wait to leave and that he desperately hoped he would be made redundant so he could go and do what he really wanted. I asked him the obvious question of what that was and he replied, 'An architect. I've always wanted to be an architect ever since I was at school.'

'So why did you go into banking?' I asked.

'As a teenager, when I told my dad that I wanted to be an architect he ridiculed me and said that it was a precarious career, too risky, that I should go into banking, because I would always have a secure job there. So I did. And regretted it every day since.'

For whatever reasons, the father had taken away his son's pen (the authorship of his own life story) and the son allowed him to do so. This is the willing or unwilling plight of literally millions of people. Some people have their pen violently removed from them, others quietly, others just give it away because they haven't decided on a story that they want to write for their lives – they have no vision, no purpose, no direction and so a quick fix, or a feel-good choice, is the one they take.

It was working in Zambia, then Uganda and Rwanda, that finally woke me up to the fact that that it doesn't matter who you are, where you're born, how little education you've had – everyone can lead their own life story, everyone can take back their life's pen. But the deeper caveat is: 'Who will benefit from my story?' This was Mandela's point when he said:

> What counts in life is not the mere fact that we have lived. It is what difference we have made to the lives of others that will determine the significance of the life we lead.

Mandela grew up in the midst of a story of oppression and segregation and injustice. He had many forces acting upon him. From within his own family he had the pressures of expectation about who he would become in the family's favoured cultural background. He was destined to become an adviser to his tribal king. There were pressures over who he should marry. He had pressures all around him from the Apartheid system, which wanted to take away his pen and the pens of all those around him so that the majority ethnicities would become the victims of someone else's story. And there was a moment where he said, 'No, this story is not fair, it is not right, it is not just, it is not humane and I don't want to support this system; it's not the story I want to write.' In that moment, he took back his pen and committed his life to writing a different story than the one family and circumstance had mapped out for him. The story he wanted to write was the story of a rainbow nation holding its head up in the world. As early as 1951, Mandela addressed the annual conference of the ANC Youth League:

> The spirit of the people cannot be crushed and no matter what happens to the present leadership, new leaders will arise like mushrooms till full victory is won.[94]

Leadership for the young Mandela didn't start out as a role, it was who he was, it was how he lived each day, it was the story he was writing. He didn't need a title to do that. Yes, the titles and roles came along later as a result of him leading himself, but they didn't make him a leader. The most common frustration I have continued to see in almost all organisations is promoting people to positions of leadership who have never even learned to lead themselves.

It's difficult to know exactly at what point in his youth Mandela truly owned his authorship. Was it his realisation that 'A black man did not have to accept the dozens of petty indignities directed at him each day',[95] or the day he escaped to Johannesburg to avoid an arranged marriage to someone he didn't love? What defined the start of him saying 'I want to write a different story for my life'?

Walter Sisulu, a Johannesburg lawyer and pivotal member of the ANC, recognised Mandela's leadership potential when the twenty-three-year-old walked into the older man's law firm. That confirms what I've now seen countless times, that we all massively benefit from someone who tells us we have the potential to be the leader of our own lives. It helps all of us to be told that we can lead ourselves and our relationships, and this will be the foundational muscle if we are ever in a leadership role. Far too many people, to repeat myself, have sought out a position of leadership without knowing how to lead themselves. They don't know how to create a personal mission, a vision for their future, how to create pathways to get themselves from where they are to where they want to be, they aren't proactive, focused or courageous, and they aren't looking at how they can be of benefit to some small part of the world.

If I could say one thing to you it would be this – you are both leaders, you are the writers of your own stories. I may give you advice, or thoughts, or input, but it's your story, not mine. You are both already proving this in the life choices you are making about your careers, what kind of family life you want to create, your values. I have great respect for you both. Keep on owning your leadership potential, nurture it, write a story that has a positive impact on the world you find yourself in. Never worry about getting a particular position or not, just make sure the story you are writing is the best one you can write that benefits others.

And remember, you guys are the bridge. You pass this vital truth on to your own children, my grandchildren, as soon as it makes sense to them – which will be soon, because kids love stories!

With love

Dad

STARTING A CONVERSATION

---

1. Where do you feel that you are writing your own life story, and where that you aren't?
2. Where do you see yourself 'giving away your pen' and how can you reclaim it?
3. If you were to be an even more effective leader of your own life, for the benefit of others, what actions would you take this week?

---

15. Grounding – discover the elusive quality of gravitas

Hi guys

How wonderful and exciting - another baby born into our family! She is so gorgeous. You have both impressed me so much with the seriousness and love with which you have entered the world of parenthood.

In the midst of all of our joy, I want to continue the conversation we started. You said the other day that Mandela was unique because he had the X factor, and that this was gravitas. I wanted to pick up on that. I think the core challenge of this conversation is whether it is possible for everyone and anyone to develop the key characteristics we saw in Mandela. Gravitas is a great example of where we instinctively think, 'No, everyone cannot develop the same virtues as Mandela.'

In my years of delivering corporate leadership coaching, I would work a lot with HR departments that were looking at who should get promoted and who shouldn't, or were putting people on performance reviews because something was missing in their performance. I would ask them why they thought this one person should be promoted, or this other person shouldn't be, or what was it that was missing in their performance. Often they would struggle to find an answer, but when they did they would frequently come up with that one word, *gravitas*. 'They don't have enough gravitas,' they would say. I would try to dig a little deeper and ask what they meant, but they couldn't articulate an answer.

The problem with gravitas is that everyone seems to know it when they see it, but finds it almost impossible to define it. My guess is that's because we see gravitas is a gift from the gods and not something we can develop. Some people definitely seem to have a certain something. They're noticed when they walk into the room; they have presence. Or when they speak at a meeting or are in a particular group, their words appear to carry more weight than other people's. There is a weight to some people's words, extra weight that results in increased impact. Or the weight may be in their very presence, or in their accumulated experiences. The more weight a person has, the more ripples, more waves, more impact, more influence they cause or possess.

Is gravitas a rare gift from the gods or does everyone has the potential for it? If they do, why don't some fulfil that potential? I'm putting my money on its being learned and not some magical halo that some people wear. What we never see is the back-story of a person's life, how they developed such gravitas. The Greeks talked about a person's *daemon* (not demon); the Romans had the same idea, but called it 'genius', the idea of a larger, deeper wind or spirit blowing through our personality. They definitely saw this as something everyone has, even if they don't recognise or work with it. I guess the million-dollar question then is how I, an average person, develop gravitas.

Like everything else we've been exploring, the answer cannot be one size fits all. Mandela's gravitas is different to Desmond Tutu's gravitas, which is different to the Dalai

Lama's gravitas, which is different to Michael Jordan's gravitas. People rarely have gravitas in every dimension of their life. So when I talk about becoming Mandela, what I really mean is becoming fully me, like he became fully him, and this will look very different and show itself in different arenas of life for each person. For some it will be at home or in the family, some at work, some in social settings, some in the sports arena and some in the spiritual or religious environment. For example, Ken Wilber is a giant when you hear him speak or write about integrative spirituality and psychology, but I can't imagine he is very confident at parties (I may be wrong, of course).

As we think through how to develop gravitas, using the idea of weight is helpful. Some people seem 'weightless', you hardly know they're there, they almost hide behind their own shadow. You wouldn't use the word 'gravitas' about people like that. Others throw their weight around, but it isn't in fact their weight, it's their ego and insecurities they are throwing around. You wouldn't use the word 'gravitas' about people like that either.

The leadership coach and writer Peter Hawkins helped me more than anyone to see how we can all develop gravitas.[96] I think we talked this through when you were interviewing for jobs last year, but let me recap. Think of a triangle like this:

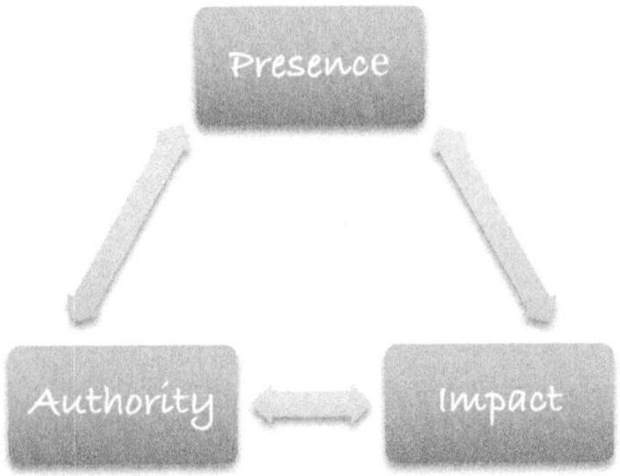

Let's start with authority. The first thing to say is that this doesn't mean authoritarian and it doesn't mean anything to do with a position in a hierarchy. Authority simply means the weight of a person's story or experience. Some people you notice that they are in the room and others you don't. Take George Roberts, who survived Idi Amin's Ugandan terror. You remember I said he was very quiet, but the moment I met him and heard his story I sensed his arresting presence. There was something about him that demanded to be listened to because of all that he had been through. It was similar when Walter Sisulu first met the young Mandela. He said he knew instantly that here was a leader who could play a vital role in the youth wing of the ANC. He must have noticed something about Mandela's words, the way he carried himself, his experience, interactions with people, convictions or character.

But what do we really mean when we say someone has authority? Where does this dimension, the weight, the gravitas come from? As I said in my last letter, authority contains the word 'author'. What real-life stories have we written so far? Often, we call this our CV or biography, a list of what we've done and what we've achieved. I've helped you both write CVs for yourselves in the past. But I'm not talking here about a piece of paper. Imagine a toolkit, like granddad's old canvas one in his garage that you used to search through. Imagine it has nothing in it: there's no weight in the bag, nothing to show and nothing that's useful. Now imagine that every experience you accumulate as you go through life is like a tool – everything you've learned formally or informally, every bit of wisdom you've gained, all the knowledge accrued and skills developed, every exam you've passed. Each one of these goes into your toolkit. Now when you pick it up, it's full of weight. The weight of *you*. That is gravitas.

As a practical step it's definitely worth writing down everything you've done, achieved, explored – a real-life CV not written for the eyes of a prospective employer, but rather for you to see and own yourself, your authority (your authorship). We have all accumulated experiences, skills, exams, learning, abilities, but we may not have owned them fully as our own. They don't feed us with confidence and courage. One of the problems for many people I've met is that they don't own their own story. They have done things, achieved things, studied things, but when they walk into the room it's like they don't bring themselves with them. They have no tools in their kit. This is the difference between people who have authority and those who don't. But I'm not talking about arrogance and ego. If someone comes into a room and they're full of themselves, it's a sign of their insecurity, the very opposite of someone who is owning their own story.

When I started working as a leadership consultant and was asked to train people in negotiation, I remember feeling inadequate. It was like my toolkit was empty in this area. I told my boss about it one day after a particular training event. I explained I had never been a negotiator and I felt a fraud teaching the subject, however good my theoretical understanding was.

He challenged me outright and told me, "Yes, you do have negotiating experience.'

'No, I don't. I've never negotiated anything,' I replied.

'Yes, you have.'

Now I was getting somewhat frustrated with him, but I let him carry on.

'You bought a house, didn't you?' he asked me.

'Yes.'

'You've bought cars before, haven't you?'

'Yes.'

'Didn't you have a conversation about agreeing a price?'

'Yes.'

'Well, what do you call that?'

I was silenced. Of course I'd negotiated before. He was right. And when I owned a few of my own negotiation stories, it reminded me of more and more experiences I'd had and so my authority as a teacher of negotiation grew. People get so linear in their understanding of what they have done or achieved. They think that because they've had one particular job, they need to stick to applying for similar kinds of jobs. But if you look at every job you've had, all the experience you've had and the studying you've done, each involved a whole stream of different skills that could be used in many different situations. These are what are called *transferable skills*. People want to be able to look at us and say:

- 'They know what they're talking about.'
- 'They've been there, done that and got the T-shirt.'
- 'They have the battle scars to prove they should be listened to.'

I learned recently the meaning of the phrase *show me your metal*. In the days when all grinding of wheat for flour was done by windmills, a range of local skills were needed, one of which was dressing the huge mill stones. You've seen them: they are massive and if one fell on you it would crush you to death. For the two great mill stones to effectively grind the wheat into flour, each stone face has a network of very fine grooves cut by master stonemasons or millwrights. This process is called 'dressing'. If a windmill needed its stones serviced and re-cut, the giant windmill sails would be placed at a certain angle and this would tell a passing millwright that there was a job for them. But how would a windmill owner know whether the millwright presenting themselves at his door was an experienced master or an inexperienced chancer? A skilled millwright has a set of fine-edged metal tools to cut the grooves and the endless hours of work would see tiny fragments of metal break off and embed themselves in their hands. So the windmill owner's interview technique was simple. He would say to the visiting millwright 'Show me your metal', meaning 'Show me your hands'. An experienced millwright would have shards of metal embedded all over his hands, while a novice would still have unblemished hands. A millwright's hands told the story of his experience – his hands were his gravitas.

We may not be true judges of our own gravitas. You may remember I did that evening course at Cambridge University on International Development many years ago. I felt totally out of my depth. I was only going along because I wanted to put some learning behind the work I was doing with the HIV charity Cherish Uganda. Well, I'd done about two terms of classes every Wednesday night and then one Saturday we had a whole day of study. I remember it well because it was a beautiful spring day. People on the course were slowly getting to know each other and so coffee break seemed a lot more friendly and relaxed than the evening sessions had been. I got talking to one woman about the course and the study day and she took me by surprise when she suddenly said, 'Actually, most of us on the course are wondering why you are here.'

As you can imagine, I was taken aback by the bluntness of that statement. I thought she was saying that no one liked me! I looked at her with a quizzical expression, busily managing my internal emotions.

She continued, 'You clearly have more experience than all of us in these areas of International Development and you could be teaching the course, not attending it.'

I was shocked. I saw myself as a kid from the country and she saw me as a person with some weight behind them.

This is what I mean about the authority dimension of gravitas. We can all develop it by truly owning in our heart and our head everything we have authored in our lives so far. No one has nothing in their toolkit. We can all pick up a reasonably full bag if we think about our experiences hard enough. The key is to have a bag full of our own stories, not the ones we think we should have. I know we often joke about 'blagging', but hubris and invention don't create gravitas. The truth does.

Going back to the triangle, another dimension of gravitas is what I'm calling *presence*, being fully present with whoever you are with at the time. This is all about relationships – one on one as well as in groups. Listening, eye contact and empathy are all part of the rhythm of presence, but it isn't all about silence. Some people come into a room and don't greet anyone, don't welcome anyone, they slide in and out unnoticed, because they have chosen to hide their presence away. Sometimes it's out of extreme introversion, but sometimes they are just plain rude. This is true of thoughts and actions as well. People with presence tell you what they are thinking, they act on what they are feeling, they ask you about your day or family or experience. They don't settle for a 'How are you? Fine, thanks' kind of conversation, they ask follow-up questions: 'What is going well for you right now?' Presence is about being engaged with another person.

Do you remember Patrick, who we met in Rwanda? I think it was our second or third visit there to a conference. When he was with us, he was never fully there: he was always distracted by his phone, or looking around to see if there was anyone he knew, or someone more important than us he could go and network with. That isn't being present. Presence is bringing all of yourself (your authority) to a conversation with another person or group of people. Presence is having a connection with others that is going to make having an impact possible. That story I told you a while back of Mandela giving children sweets, one child at a time, is an act of presence. Be with the person you are with, be in the meeting you are at, don't be distracted by phones and iPads or side conversations. I watch mums walking their kids to school these days and many are not present with their kids, they are too busy on their phones.

The third and final dimension of gravitas is *impact*. If authority is bringing all of yourself into the room and presence is fully connecting and engaging with others, then impact is using your energy to move the people you are talking to in the direction of meaningful action. Impact is the actual effect or influence that you have on another person. Whether it's leaving them feeling good, or affirmed, or connecting to their sense of purpose or mission, or whether it's an action they are seeking, someone with impact makes sure there *is* an outcome to the conversation. It may simply be the impact of the person being left with a feeling of being understood, or cared for, or listened to in a way that empowers them (puts power into them) or encourages them (puts courage into them).

I've struggled with the issue of impact more than the other two. I've had a faulty belief that if I could bring myself into the room (authority) and be fully present with whoever or whatever is going on there (presence), then there would automatically be some kind of outcome, people would know what to do or just be motivated to do something. But then I'd be disappointed when nothing changed. I make this big assumption about my impact, but what I fail to do is follow through to a conclusion, to state 'This is what I'd love to see happen here' or 'Could you please do X?' or 'What will you do now?' I shouldn't assume that people will take action, but instead get clear and help others get clear about where they will go next. This is true in relationships and private life as well as at work. When we have impact, we can shift the emotional balance in a conversation, we can open up new ideas and possibilities, we can take things in a new direction. We can make something happen. Gravitas has these three dimensions and we can learn all three.

I've been thinking lately how important it is to set your sails early in life. Like we set the sails of a boat to make it head off in a certain direction, we get ourselves into habits early in life that will increase our gravitas or not. Setting the sails to a passionate purpose, to improving our heart and character, to authority, presence and impact – all of these lead us towards greater gravitas as a person. I'm well aware that the things we do now are often rooted in some early habits. It is so easy to arrive in your early thirties having gone from college straight into a demanding job, taking on a big mortgage and then suddenly, maybe when a new baby arrives, put your head above water for a few minutes and ask yourself, maybe for the first time, 'Is this the life I really want?' But by then your sails are set in a particular direction and while it's not impossible, for most of us changing course is too much of a challenge. So developing gravitas needs to start young.

Maybe I'm naïve, but I live with the idealistic hope that this is one area in which 'olders' could help 'youngers' in thinking through these issues. But that of course assumes that the older has carried on growing themselves!

I would really value your thoughts on all of this, particularly that last point.

Much love

Dad

STARTING A CONVERSATION

1. Take one key life experience and think through all of the skills and attributes that you used to navigate it.
2. Who do you know personally who has gravitas? What is it they do or say, or how do they behave, that makes you think this?
3. Looking at the three dimensions of gravitas (authority, presence and impact), rate yourself on each one (10 being strong) and come up with a few actions to strengthen the weaker scores.

16. Discipline – exercise in the daily gym of life

Hi guys

I recently read Mandela's book *Dare Not Linger*,[97] in which he talks about what happened after he became President of South Africa. You'll remember the famous words in the final pages of his autobiography that gave the title to the book, 'I have walked that long walk to freedom', but a lot of people stop at that sentence and don't read on to the end:

> I have discovered the secret that after climbing a great hill, one only finds that there are many more hills to climb. I have taken a moment to rest, to steal a view of the glorious vista that surrounds me, to look back on the distance I have come. But I can rest only for a moment, for with freedom come responsibilities and I dare not linger, for my long walk is not yet ended.[98]

He published those words in 1994 at the age of seventy-four, and his wife, Graça Machel, had them republished four years after his death. The message he was conveying is that life is a struggle; life itself is a continuous long walk to freedom. Life is a continual struggle for liberation, justice and mutual relationships. The liberation journey is the deep structure of the universe for each one of us who pass through it. Mandela was saying that now we have ended Apartheid politically, we need to move the struggle for justice into every aspect of our society, government, health, education and environment, but even more importantly to continue the liberation struggle within each person's own heart and character.

I find this so challenging, because it forces me to confront my own inner racism, discrimination and injustice, my own inner terrorist, oppressor and aggressor. This is the struggle, the long walk to freedom, that lies before every human being.

I was chatting with my friend Lennox the other day. I've told you about him before. He grew up in Apartheid South Africa and has remained committed to the enormous challenges that still exist, particularly among young people. We were discussing *Dare Not Linger* and he told me that one of the challenges for South Africa, post 1994, was the false feeling that the struggle was over. The feeling that we've reached the mountaintop and deserve comfort now, we are entitled to all of the spoils of freedom – but without the responsibilities, without the struggle. Young black people, understandably, demanded a share in the land that had made the white people so rich. But they didn't want the discipline of getting up at six o'clock to plough the fields, do the back-breaking weeding, the farm management challenges, deal with the water problems and the pestilence, let alone having to find the markets to sell in. It isn't just a problem in South Africa. I can see this same problem of entitlement everywhere. I see parents in the UK are desperate to make life easier for their children than they had it when they were young. They seek to remove all discomfort, they don't want their children to have to experience hardship, and they think that this is love. In reality they are stealing one of the two foundation stones for children to make their life journey – the deep knowledge of self-worth and the ability to continue to struggle well. I sympathise with this, as you will also sympathise, because you are now parents of your own children. We want to make life easier for our kids, because that seems to be the loving thing to do.

Let me dwell a little longer on the idea of struggle being seen as the norm in our lives. Why do I have to struggle? There is something about the words *hard*, *tough* and *struggle* that are very unappealing. Who wants a view of adult life as one of struggle? Your uncle worked extremely hard for forty-five years and is on the cusp of retiring and he doesn't want to have to struggle to work out how to live a meaningful life for the next twenty years. That wasn't a struggle he was expecting, or had prepared for.

We want to stop life being tough. We want comfort. We want ease.

Why? Because ease is the natural state and the reward for being human. Our view of life's journey is that it's a period of necessary struggle that results in relief and an end to effort. The imaginary default of life is that it should be unchallenging and struggle is seen as an anomaly. We work in order to get to a place of rest where life is less demanding, not just briefly but so we can linger. This is the false narrative we tell ourselves.

It has taken me years to understand this, but I now see that the journey to personal and societal liberation is itself a struggle. Full stop. Struggle is the norm of being human. It never ends. That's not a note of pessimism, it's a note of fact. That's just how it is. For example, doing stretching exercises every morning is a struggle, but if I don't do them my body will atrophy. The wrestling with my ego, my selfishness, my self-doubts, my limitations – real or imagined - along with my own inner oppressor, dictator, racist and terrorist, all of these continue across my life span. None of these struggles ends when we reach forty or fifty or sixty or even seventy. All of the inner struggles carry on, along with the daily struggle with the challenges of our external circumstances. Life happens, events happen, and as a result we react. Do we do nothing and simply let life shape our inner and outer worlds, or do we respond, take action, weed the garden of our heart, confront our sense of entitlement or other oppressive voices? Struggle is part of building anything that is worth building, it is part of creating our life as a unique work of art, and it is part of our life's journey.

Doing nothing merely creates a different kind of struggle. Leaving my attitudes unchecked, my thought patterns unchallenged, my body unexercised, my mind unfed, my character undeveloped, my heart unstretched leaves room for entropy and atrophy. Untended gardens grow wild and fill up with weeds that choke out the potential good things. Undeveloped hearts and minds become entitled and small and trivial.

Struggle is the necessary response to becoming more fully human. As with anything good in life, it doesn't happen by accident. Struggle simply means effort. I make a daily effort with my heart, mind, character, body and attitudes to ensure that I continue on my own long walk to freedom.

That brings me to the word *discipline*. It takes discipline to struggle well each day. But how on earth do you make the word discipline attractive? How do you sugar-coat it so you take the medicine? No one signs up for courses on discipline. Discipline for me was naturally associated with punishment. We were told to discipline our kids by the parenting gurus and what they meant was smack them, tell them off, sit them on the naughty step. There was no 'good juice' in the word. When they looked at someone else's badly behaved children, people quietly said to each other that the parents obviously didn't discipline their kids. The focus was on the judgement of bad behaviour, or giving a message of pain to curb that behaviour. It's hard to get past these old ghosts or echoes of discomfort, pain, horsehair shirts and cold showers in the morning. Even when we weren't being disciplined (read 'punished'), our parents were often trying to raise us up with their values – sit still, eat with your mouth closed, eat with both knife and fork, clean your teeth twice a day. There was good and bad in all they sought to teach us and eventually we had to sift through what were their values and what are ours.

What I'm talking about here is what is called self-discipline. Maybe if I used a different word – exercise – that would work. In the Greek of the New Testament, discipline is connected to the word 'exercise',[99] which has a similar root to our word for training, or gymnasium. Discipline is where we go to get fit for life. It's like life's gymnasium. Of course, when you look at it like that it makes more sense. We don't go to the gym for the sake of it, we don't exercise for the sake of it, we exercise so we can be more effective at life. If I want to run for the bus, I need to practise running so I'm fit enough; if I want to lessen my risk of heart disease, I need to practise good daily eating habits; if I want to develop the gift of a focused mind, I need to practise meditation each day. Whatever I want to do with my life, I need to know I have a fit enough muscle memory to deliver it. You guys know this. You run three or four times a week because you want your body to be ready for the next half-marathon. Discipline for you is a necessity, it isn't a dirty word.

Mandela was a man of discipline. He learned it, he practised it, so that when he called upon his body, his mind, his spirit to do something, the mind, body or spirit was fit and ready to respond. An article in *Newsweek* in 1990 described Mandela's discipline as his secret weapon.[100] What did he do each day? He set himself a punishing physical daily routine, even in jail, to keep himself physically strong. He set himself the daily mental discipline of serious academic study and encouraged his fellow prisoners to do the same. He set himself the moral discipline each day of speaking kindly to those who mistreated him. He set himself the spiritual discipline of 15–20 minutes of meditation every day to check that his own spirit did not become embittered and his character was worthy of the leader of a nation. His focus on discipline wasn't an accident, it was intentional. Discipline was a value that he held strongly. He himself said:

> Human beings like to be associated with a hard-working, disciplined & successful person &, by carefully cultivating these qualities, you will win yourself many friends.[101]

Mandela saw the connection between discipline and leadership and held no punches when he addressed the youth of South Africa two months after his release from prison in 1990:

> As future leaders there are certain responsibilities which we expect you to observe. One of these is utmost discipline. If you are not disciplined, you can never win our confidence.[102]

My own experience is that there are some areas I find it easier to be disciplined in than others, and some of those have changed over the years. Sometimes it takes a shock to make us start the daily disciplines of life. My friend Colin was diagnosed with diabetes a year ago. It was a total shock, but it also galvanised him. He set himself eating targets and exercise targets and got his weight down and the diabetes under control. Someone described these kinds of shocks as a *severe mercy*. They are like a painful wake-up and a second chance.

One of my wake-up calls in recent years led me to the daily practice of meditation. I was working in Nairobi, Kenya, in 2013 when it was particularly unsafe, and then moved to live in South Africa. I had felt the tension getting inside my head and my body and kept on trying to tough it out. I remember around Easter sitting in an armchair early one morning, on the vineyard we were living at in Paarl, saying to myself, 'If you don't find a different way to handle all this stress, it is going to kill you.' So I started that morning to discover daily meditation and have done it pretty much every day since. I don't do it just for fun: I have a larger sense of my life depending on it, a bigger reason than merely a habit I've fallen into.

An interview with Mandela in *Newsweek* sums up what I'm saying:

> He (Mandela) is a man whose life instructs us that people can assert control of their personal destiny no matter what the force of the hardships they incur and that they can, by their own conduct, overwhelm the odds against them.[103]

It's so easy to write about all of this, but the wake-up slapped me again when I told Jane I was writing to you guys about discipline. She asked me, 'Do you think you are a disciplined person? Where are you disciplined? Where aren't you disciplined?' I felt myself crash-land yet again on the airfield of reality, and the need to go look at myself in the mirror once more.

Much love

Dad

STARTING A CONVERSATION

1. Are you a disciplined person? Where are you disciplined? Where aren't you disciplined?
2. If there was one discipline you needed in order to get your life to where you want it to go, what discipline would you start today?
3. What mindset do you need to develop that will ensure you can keep up a daily discipline in your life? What is the mini battle you need to name and win?

17. Forgiveness – practise the art of being human

Hi guys

I was talking about you both to a friend of mine in Kenya last week and discussing the idea of becoming Mandela. To start with I didn't think the conversation added much to what I'd already been considering, but over the days that followed I found my mind turning over some thoughts I haven't explored with you yet. I've talked to you before about the dangers of seeing Mandela as a hero, because heroes become something distant to our experience, unattainable, like trophies put on pedestals to admire. What I haven't explored is the opposite of being a hero, which is simply the art of being human. We're all human and heroes are humans too, who can hopefully inspire us to aspire to be our best selves. But being human is also about being made of clay. Philosophers from the Apostle Paul through to Leonard Cohen have reminded us that we are all cracked vessels. We are all a mix of glorious and flawed skills and character. In fact, in the ancient art of *kintsugi*, it is the very flaws and cracks of the broken pots that are celebrated, through the use of gold, to create something beautiful.[104]

In the first half of my life it was hard to welcome my own humanness. I wanted to succeed, to achieve, gain some kind of standing, reputation, respect, be in control – not particularly in a famous, well-known kind of way, but in such a way that I could privately feel good about myself. I also wanted to be the good guy, the moral guy, the faithful guy, the person of exemplary character. I worked so hard to present this polished version of myself to the world that I actually came to believe it was true. I hid the cracks even from myself.

And then came the fall.

It surprised you, but it equally surprised me. It wasn't that I was deceiving the world, it was that I was deceiving myself. I hadn't owned my clay feet, my humanity. I came face to face, in a painful way, with the truth about myself and it wasn't a private viewing, it was on display for all to see. And the biggest crime, if that's the right word, was not being honest with myself about myself.

What I learned was that there are things in one's humanity that are plain wrong. Things like lying and stealing and physical or emotional abuse or violence – all of the character flaws that break the trust of the people around you. But there are also unavoidable crashes, failures you can't escape. Like driving down the road in the dark and a deer rushes out in front of you and leaves you no time to avoid it. Either way there will be a car crash. Everything within you abhors the thought of killing an animal and yet, at the same time, your self-preservation knows you will kill yourself if you crash off the road in trying to avoid hitting it.

When we consider Mandela's life, there are some obvious things about him that reveal his flawed humanity. His ego, his anger, his broken relationships, his pedantic traits, his self-confessed policy failures. These are the aspects of himself that he worked on, starting in prison, including his views about violent versus non-violent struggle to end Apartheid.

However, there were other revelations of his humanity that are much more complex – what I am calling the unavoidable failures. Thirty years ago I might have disagreed with what I'm writing, but these thoughts come from my own painful experiences. I observe the same in Mandela. Mandela left his first wife. Looked at from one perspective, what he did was abandonment and unfaithfulness. It's hard to argue against that view. Yet his first wife didn't want him to get increasingly involved in the liberation struggle, she wanted him at home with her and the children; a response from her that is totally understandable. From Mandela's perspective, he was deeply conflicted. He had a deep call, a vocation, to lead liberation within the nation. A deep sense of injustice called to him from all he saw and he needed to respond whatever the cost. History would look at this and possibly cheer him on. What was he to do? Stay at home and not fulfil his vocation? Fulfil his vocation and damage his wife and children? He chose to leave. This is what I mean by an unavoidable failure. If he had chosen to stay, you would never have heard of Nelson Mandela and who knows what would have happened to him, or his marriage, or South Africa.

These kinds of decisions, decisions that involve the impossible, 'damned if you do, damned if you don't' choices, are the unavoidable car crashes of our humanity. It's no good trying to justify them in terms of right or wrong, or by how the story turned out. At the time you have no idea what the actual consequences will be. Such decisions can be neither justified nor vilified. A rabbi friend of mine told me recently that his tradition's view is to acknowledge the complex mess of the choices made, but then to take responsibility for the outcome without trying to hide it or justify it. To look oneself in the mirror and say 'I am human', not as an excuse, but as a statement of acceptance.

And what of Mandela's marriage to Winnie? She was supportive of his political vocation and the life of struggle it committed him to, but she and their marriage paid the price in a different way than his first marriage. From the start he was either on the run or in prison. She herself was shamed and tortured for her association with him. The government powers thought they could defeat Mandela by terrorising his wife and family. Was she weak for her eventual unfaithfulness, or was she also just human? We want categories, we want it to be clear who are the good guys and the bad guys, we want clear lines drawn and no colouring over the lines. What we don't want of our heroes is their rich and complex humanity.

Maybe, as I have increasingly reflected, there is a deeper truth underlying our humanity that helps us make sense of all of our messes – the clear ones and the unavoidable ones. This deeper truth of humanity is forgiveness. Forgiving oneself and forgiving others are how we take ownership of our messy humanity and create a pathway to move on.

I used to have a pretty flimsy view of forgiveness – it wasn't much more than a quick 'I'm sorry' and then you're done. The writings of therapist Dan Allender gave me my first true insight into this. He says that real forgiveness is a two-stage process. First, you need to face up to the full damage that has been done – either the damage and hurt you did to others, or what they did to you. The key is not to minimise or rationalise the hurt that has been done, but also not to get stuck there, because the second part of the process is the choice not to make the person responsible pay for what they've done. You don't make things nicer, but you do choose to open, or keep open, the doorway to a relationship. And it starts with forgiving yourself.

Mandela was only too aware of the pain his choices had caused to his first wife, to his children, to his second wife, to their children and to his mother, who probably never really understood why he had given over his life to the cause of ending the depths of injustice that had become hardwired into their country. Because of his choices he could not be at the funerals of his son, or his mother, or protect his wife Winnie against the actions of the police. To forgive himself was the only route to a continued path of personal growth and fulfilling his vocation. He had to identify all of the impacts of his choices by name, call them out for what they were and what they did, and then choose not to make himself pay through self-loathing, self-destructive thoughts, self-defeat and self-punishment. Forgiveness opens up a conversation and it opens up the possibility of a new day, of walking forwards and of making new and different choices.

Discovering how to forgive yourself is the only way to be able to forgive others. On top of the years of Apartheid oppression at every level of his life, Mandela's prison years were characterised by repeated abuse, shaming, humiliation, and physical and mental oppression – all of which was dehumanising. What explains his persistent humanity to his oppressors? He didn't pretend their abuses were any less awful than they were, he didn't ever let his oppressors off the hook for what they were doing, but he chose not to make them pay. He met their lack of humanity with interest, respect and concern. It was his ability to forgive others that opened the door to a conversation with his oppressors at a time when those around him counselled him that this was a weakness and a compromise, or even capitulation. And it was his choice to forgive that created the pathway towards ending Apartheid. Without the courage to forgive, there would have been no genuine route available. Forgiveness for Mandela was an act of leadership. In a conversation with Richard Stengel he once said:

> I am working now with the same people who threw me into jail, persecuted my wife, hounded my children from one school to the other… and I am one of those who is saying, 'let us forget the past and think of the present'.[105]

Because he was reconciled with his own messy humanity, he was able to reconcile himself to the messy humanity of his oppressors.

The core of this lesson that to be human is to forgive – oneself and then others – was reflected in the establishment of the Truth and Reconciliation Commission[106] under the chairmanship of Archbishop Desmond Tutu. The very words Truth and Reconciliation sum up the two stages of Allender's process of forgiveness:

- Truth – face up, with unvarnished honesty, to the damage done.
- Reconciliation – choose to offer an open hand to a new, or renewed, relationship with both yourself and others.

I find it interesting that the major religions talk about forgiveness as something very spiritual, when actually it is essentially and necessarily very human. But then maybe that is what 'spiritual' truly means – being truly human. That's why I'm coming to the conclusion that forgiveness, as a foundational or transcendent skill, is the essence, the art of being human.

I am very aware as I write this letter to you that it is easy to talk about Mandela and forgiveness in a way that I could easily hide behind, rather than open up the conversation about what this means for us and all that we have been through together.

I'm happy to talk this through with you when you're ready.

Much love

Dad

STARTING A CONVERSATION

1. Talk about a time when you found it hard to forgive. Why was this and what helped you to move forwards?
2. What relationships are hard for you to hold open the door to right now, and how can you help yourself to keep working on those relationships?
3. Take one of the most inspiring examples you have seen of someone offering forgiveness and humanity. What are the lessons you can learn from them?

18. Ubuntu – see everything through a different lens

Hi guys

When you were very young, I used to religiously watch the American TV series *NYPD Blue*. Detective Sipowicz (Dennis Franz) had this wonderful one-liner he often used: *everything is a situation*. It was his way of trying to explain to someone, in the simplest way he knew, how you can look at an incident and make a judgement as to what happened, but it probably won't be the right judgement. Why? Because everything is surrounded by a context that is always a lot more complex and multidimensional than the incident itself.

Remember that famous image in a newspaper where the photo showed someone seemingly being attacked by a thug? When the whole context was revealed, it showed some masonry falling from a high building that was going to hit the passerby – the young man saw what was happening and shoved the person out of danger. In the close-up shot he looks like a thug, in the wide-angle shot he's revealed to be a hero. Everything is a situation. The lens through which you see life controls your view. If you change your lens you may, as the detective was trying to illustrate, end up with a totally different reading of the situation.

Back in 2006, when we first visited Rwanda, I realised that if I had been travelling with someone other than you, it would have been a totally different experience. We achieved all we did on that trip because we both wanted to have the richest experience we could. If I'd been with someone who wanted to lie in bed, have meals on time, have certainty about our itinerary, then it would have been a very different trip. What it made me appreciate too is that who we travel through life with shapes who we become and how we end up living in the world. *It matters who you travel with.*

So what have my *NYPD* and Rwanda 'mantras' got to do with this idea of who we are becoming? It has a lot to do with who Mandela became and therefore I think it's vital for this conversation we're having. I said a few letters ago that elders shaped Mandela's life from the beginning to the end. His relationship with elders was the 'X factor' in who he became. But the whole idea of elders sits within a view of society and culture generally that is very different to the one I see around me today. Where are the elders around me, or you, who will shape our journey? Is my ambition to see the growth of elders in our society actually impossible? The world we are in, the context, the lens through which we develop our ideas and our institutions are based on Western consumer individualism. The American dream, as it is called, is essentially an individualistic and consumeristic ideal. Mandela's life was shaped by a very different perspective.

When I first started researching and exploring around elders, I was invited to present some of my early thoughts to a group at University College London. As I was concluding my talk, I distinctly remember a young Indian woman standing up and very graciously telling me that I had only got a Western person's view on the issue. I invited her to explain what she meant to the group. She told us that when she went to university it wasn't *her* going, it was her whole village. She saw herself as an extension of, a representative of, her family and her village. For her there was both collective pride and collective responsibility. The same was true when she got married. She embraced her future through the lens of the whole community, not just as a family or personal event. The perspective through which she saw the world, a more Eastern or ancient cultural view, was that life is not about me, it's about *us*, not my identity but *our* identity, not my success but *our* success, not my prosperity but *our* prosperity. The deep idea that forms this lens is that my identity, my sense of who I am, of where I belong, of my personal meaning in life, is inextricably bound up in us, we, our community.

I am because we are. This is the fundamental philosophy that undergirded all of Mandela's childhood, youth, community, society. Every breath Mandela breathed, every step he took, was shaped by a deep sense of *us*, not of I. In African cultural history this is called ubuntu. Desmond Tutu describes Mandela's worldview in this way:

> Ubuntu... speaks of the very essence of being human... It is to say, 'My humanity is caught up, is inextricably bound up, in yours'. We belong in a bundle of life. We say, 'A person is a person through other persons'.[107]

It is thought that the only reason Mandela managed to end Apartheid was because he lived from a worldview of ubuntu. No one got what they individually wanted in order that *everyone* got what they wanted – peace and justice.[108]

What does this mean for us? It means that our identity, who we are becoming, is not individualistic, it is communal. Who I am is shaped through my relationships.

Actually, this is so important that I want to make the point even stronger. We cannot become who we really are on our own. It's impossible.

Let me try to unpick this thought. When I was cycle racing as a teenager, I worked very hard, I trained every day and I raced every weekend. I got good. It was at that point that I was offered a coach. The purpose of a coach is to take you from good to best. It's no coincidence that all top-level sports people have a coach. The principle is clear in life, as in sport – you cannot be your best on your own. In helping us in our becoming, people cannot live our lives for us, but they can walk the road with us; they can't make our problems go away, but they can provide strength, wisdom, encouragement and a sounding board. This is how we become our own version of Mandela.

'It matters who you travel with' is a challenge to our individualism, our heroic idea of 'I did it my way' or 'I did it on my own'. This communal thinking is a conscious shift in life lens. The lesson from Mandela is very clear: he utterly relied on who he travelled with. We've already seen that he travelled with elders across his whole life. We also touched on the fact that he surrounded himself with friends who had no fear about calling him out on his ego, his motives and his actions. He didn't travel with 'yes men' or 'yes women'. Even from his early days as an outsider arriving in Johannesburg he describes this:

> As a result of these (Lazar Sidelsky and John Mngoma) and other contacts I made during my early days in Johannesburg, I developed some inner strength and soon forgot about my difficulties and my poverty and suffering, my loneliness and frustrations. These connections gave me the confidence that I could

> stand on my own two feet, enjoy the goodwill and support of worthy men and women I had not previously known and to whom I could turn in case of need.[109]

The roots of the changes within him, the roots of the statesman he became, can be traced back to right here, to the people he was travelling with. In my experience this doesn't happen by accident. You have to call the right people alongside of you. I've started working with a new mentor recently and it took two years to find the right person. I've had a great coach in the past few years, but I had to ask him to take that role in my life. Starting the process of pulling the right people alongside needs you to reach out first. My advice, if I may give it, is never wait for the right people to come to you – always seek them out. I read a comment from the artist Charlie Mackesy[110] last week, where one of his characters in his new book asks a friend this question: 'What is the bravest thing you've ever done?' To which the reply was, 'Asked for help.'

But more than that, we need a team around us. We all do. Mandela became Mandela because he had a team around him. If we take a look at the intense twenty-seven-year classroom of his imprisonment, the petri dish that absolutely shaped who he became, then it's quite clear that he only survived because of the team he had around him. He did not survive alone. In his own words:

> Prison is designed to break one's spirit and destroy one's resolve. To do this, the authorities attempt to exploit every weakness, demolish every initiative, negate all signs of individuality—all with the idea of stamping out that spark that makes each of us human and each of us who we are. Our survival depended on understanding what the authorities

> were attempting to do to us, and sharing that understanding with each other. It would be very hard, if not impossible, for one man alone to resist. I do not know that I could have done it had I been alone. But the authorities' greatest mistake was keeping us together, for together our determination was reinforced. We supported each other and gained strength from each other.[111]

So who is on my team? Who is on your team? Who do we need to surround ourselves with to ensure that we root our identity in an 'us' rather than a 'me' view of the world? Who do we need on our team to ensure that we find the friends, mentors, elders who will support, challenge and grow us in heart, character, worldview, spirituality, mission? The longer I have journeyed, the more people I feel I need on my team. Apart from Jane, I need friends, I need sharp thinkers and experts, but I need a coach, I need a mentor, I need a therapist, I need elders, I need a spiritual director. I also need people like my chiropractor and a good doctor on the health side. I need people for feedback, people who have been down the track I'm on, people who will challenge me, people I trust, people who compensate for the narrowness of my worldview and experiences. You need to assemble your own team too.

But there's something even more than who I walk with and who are part of 'team me'. It's an even deeper issue I'm struggling to explain, probably because I'm still trying to understand it myself. It's about my actual identity. We can have friends, even a team, surrounding us to help us become our best. But the deeper truth that Mandela understood is that my identity is not individualistic. I am not just me, an island amid a few billion other islands – I am 'us', I am 'we'. I do not only belong to something greater than myself, who I am, my identity, is actually a part of others. Others carry a part of me and I carry a part of them. We cannot complete our own jigsaw puzzle without the missing pieces other people hold. The poet John Donne so clearly captured this in his poem 'No Man Is an Island':

> No man is an island entire of itself; every man
> is a piece of the continent, a part of the main...
> ...any man's death diminishes me,
> because I am involved in mankind.

I am not completely 'me' on my own. I am a piece of a larger whole and all the other pieces of that larger whole are a part of me. It is no accident that Gandhi understood this, Martin Luther King understood this and Mandela understood this. Their stature as elders came from the fact they knew that who they were was part of something more than them. By letting go of the individualistic self, they actually became not smaller, but much larger people in the world. So fully becoming 'me' involves letting go of myself, losing myself. This is a universal truth shared by all the major world religions. It is the deeper, call it spiritual, but fundamentally human dimension of becoming my version of Mandela. I lose myself, my solo ego-centred self, to become part of something more than me, and in that I find myself in a different, larger way.

If that thought doesn't make your brain fry, then I haven't expressed my point well. The challenge for us in particular is that we are Western. Me, you, your kids – we are shaped by the individualistic worldview we have drunk from since we were born. Mandela and half the world have drunk from a different well. They grew up seeing identity as communal. The reason this makes my brain ache is that I now have to ask how I can possibly begin to think about myself, my life, my becoming through these new eyes.

I've been listening to the speeches of Martin Luther King recently. In his speech on the American dream he says, 'We must start our thinking globally.'[112] We must begin to look at any situation through the eyes of an interdependent 'us', all of us, the whole-world-us, if we are to make sense of it and act wisely in helping ourselves. He underlined that I cannot forge my identity by starting with *me* and *I*. As I said, this is a challenge for me. I am trying to work out how to begin to rethink who I am becoming in relation to the reality of ubuntu. Where I see it helping me is in owning that I am unique, but I am not special. I'm a leaf in the vineyard, a wave in the ocean. I belong, because I belong to a greater reality that was there before I was born and will exist after I die. Owning ubuntu as I grow older is helping me to frame death and ageing too.

There is so much to talk about here. Let's arrange a Skype or a visit very soon.

Much love

Dad

STARTING A CONVERSATION

1. Who is on your life team and what role does each person play for you?
2. Think about interdependence and how your life is a part of my life. What benefits does this give you – and me?
3. How do you understand your identity (who you are) through the eyes of ubuntu?

CALLED TO LIVE

19. Disruptive conversations – a call to learn

Hi guys

That was a hard week between us. But if the past week taught me anything, it's that until we learn to have the *hard* conversations, we won't know how to really handle the *important* conversations.

A new phrase, or word set, is sneaking into the English language. I've noticed it in myself already and I noticed it in you too. Just as the word 'like' has now become a part of every sentence – 'It's like, you know, like when your mum asked you, like, if you would help with the dishes and you said, like, you have to, like, be kidding' – the new contender for the vernacular of the year award is actually one word repeated three times: 'Yeah yeah yeah'. The key is to say it three times very quickly, 'Yeah-yeah-yeah', in order to have the desired effect.

'Yeah-yeah-yeah' is used to nicely, but bluntly, tell the person who is talking to shut up. 'Yeah-yeah-yeah' means 'I know what you're going to say before you even say it, so you don't need to finish your sentence'.

In our relationship it means 'Dad, you have nothing new to teach me on this issue'. It means 'I know, so shut up'. I'm being frank, but that's the effect it has.

I'm trying to address a difficulty I see in the relationship between us and between the generations. We shut each other down. We're all guilty of it. I hear my generation using phrases like 'What you should do is...' and I hear your generation saying 'Yeah-yeah-yeah'. It has the same effect. We stop each other talking. We shut down the possibility of a meaningful conversation. We don't listen to each other. It used to be called the generation gap, but really that was an excuse for what is, in essence, a communication gap. Because we don't listen to each other, we don't learn from each other, and so consequently we're not comfortable having difficult conversations with each other about things that matter and on which we may have different views. We have to talk about this before I get into the conversation I really want to have with you, because what I'm aware of is that to get out from underneath the conversations we've been having, to get to what I'm going to call the 'learning conversation', will require disruption. And who wants disruption?

When we met the other day, our conversation started where most conversations do – in a safe place. We caught up on the facts and updated each other on the events of the past few weeks. It's normal to start conversations there, isn't it? It's what we do, it's what we've learned, and it's the social convention. But if that's all we ever did, then we wouldn't have grown our relationship in the way I think we have. It would be trivial, functional, neither nurturing nor challenging; if I dare use the word, it would become boring.

Psychologist M Scott Peck called this pseudocommunity, or pseudoconversation. (I was greatly helped by his work years ago, his bestseller *The Road Less Travelled*, as well as some very important thoughts on how to develop learning conversations in his books *A Different Drum* and *A World*

Waiting to Be Born.) Most conversations start out with the possibility of being real, but soon can become plastic.

As I write, I'm thinking of that incident between us last week. We could have pretended it didn't happen. We could have whitewashed over our feelings: the anger, the hurt, the frustration, the feelings of being misunderstood, of being controlled, the desire to get into a verbal fight and the desire to back off. All of these emotions were, I'm pretty sure, flooding around inside of us and we could have pretended. For a few minutes we did pretend, but why was it so tempting to do this? Because the alternative is painful, it's chaotic, it's disruptive. I could get hurt, you could get hurt. It would have got messy. We didn't know how it would have ended between us. Disruption and chaos would have broken out and something within my, and I think our, script says we should avoid this disruption at all costs.

Yet there is a cost, a huge cost, to avoiding the chaos of honest conversations: the cost of growing a false relationship, a distant relationship, a limited space for us to grow together and learn together. I have found that avoiding the chaos closes down the learning conversation. Painful though it was, I'm pleased that we didn't avoid the disruption. But it wasn't easy, for me certainly and I imagine for you as well. I could see all the old weapons coming out from our arsenals: trying to fix each other, convert the other to our viewpoint, wrestling out the 'I am right and you are wrong' confessions, along with the desire to try to heal and make things better. It was hard and I had to fight that impulse in myself to cycle back to safe and familiar pseudoconversation. But we didn't. We hung on in there.

Then there was silence between us. We'd exhausted our tactics and were left with an awkward void. In that silence, when I had stopped the self-justifying voice inside my head, I could see that I didn't really understand how the issues felt for you. I didn't really see your perspective. I didn't want to see it, because I'd been so busy trying to be right, trying to get you to agree with my point of view. It sounds crass, but I'd wanted to be the winner in the conversation, when in fact in this conversation we were both looking like losers.

In the silence I got to look at you, actually look you in the eyes. I saw a glimpse of what it was like to be misunderstood and so I stopped trying to win and just listened. I listened in order to learn. Peck called this place in a learning conversation *emptiness* – because that's what it is. No longer are we filling the space between us with a barrage of toxic self-banter, we are empty, not knowing what to say or do. The greatest challenge at this point is not to walk away or fight, but to bear the agonising impasse and discomfort of the emptiness.

This gnawing void between us of not knowing what to say or do or think is where the listening began. It's where the empathy was woken up. It's where we actually started to own our differences and accept them; and once they were accepted, we could start to explore them. It became a learning conversation. We had touched a place of grace and acceptance. We had started growing something new between us, something that was no longer your truth, or my truth, but rather a shared understanding and acceptance of all we didn't know about each other, and a willingness to learn. The space between us had grown, rather than become smaller, as is the case with repeated cycles of pseudoconversations. This is the learning conversation I think we discovered again the other day.

It wasn't our first journey through the tunnel of chaos, into emptiness and into the learning space, and I'm sure, I hope, it won't be our last. This is what keeps our relationship growing. There is no growth without having this kind of vulnerability between us and there is no vulnerability without courage. Courage to move beyond superficial conversations, courage to disrupt things between us for a short while, courage to stay in the chaos rather than rush for safe cover, courage to sit with the emptiness until we start learning from each other.

I don't think the challenge of the tough conversation we had last week is any different to the conversation I'd love to see between the generations. We, you and I, just reflected a wider issue between my peers and your peers, my generation and your generation. As I said earlier, it's a communication gap, rather than a generation gap. A generation gap sounds unresolvable because it focuses on age differences that can never be reduced. The age gap will never close, but the gap in our conversations can most definitely be closed with a little courage to undergo some disruption. If we could learn to have this kind of conversation, how could we then feed or nurture them? How could we encourage a shared conversation about things that really matter to both of us?

Now that we have learned again this past week how to have a difficult conversation, my hope is that we can use that skill to have one of the important conversations I think it would be good for us to have. The conversation I want to have with you, with your generation, with my generation, is over 'Where are all the elders?' and 'How can we both become one?'

Are you up for it?

Love

Dad

STARTING A CONVERSATION

1. Recall a difficult conversation you have had in the past. In what ways did you and your relationship grow through it?
2. Review the four phases of a disruptive conversation (pseudo - chaos - emptiness - learning) from examples in your own experience. What do you notice?
3. What are the disruptive conversations with yourself and others that you are avoiding having in your life right now?

20. Apologies – a call to clean up

Hi guys

I wrote last time about learning to have hard conversations. One of the toughest things we ever do in life is to say 'I'm sorry. I was wrong'. The ego hates being wrong and, even more, it hates having to admit it!

I was having a long conversation with my friend Brendan yesterday about what's going on in the world. We talked about everything from politics to pandemics. We knew we were indulging in a good moan, but at the end of it I said, 'I don't want to leave it there. If we don't do something, we will just become another bit of noise.' Mandela wasn't a moaner, Edith Eger isn't a moaner, David Attenborough isn't a moaner, Jane Goodall isn't a moaner. They all took responsibility for what they saw needed to change and they all acted on their convictions to make change happen. Elders are people who have developed their responsibility muscle. The word 'responsibility' is made up of two parts: response and ability. So responsibility is really the ability to respond. And being able to apologise sits at the foundation of taking responsibility.

What I have slowly come to realise is that whatever I do, my life is constantly having an impact on the world around me. My thoughts are having an impact on my own mood, my body and my emotions. My actions and attitudes are having an impact on all my relationships. There are no neutral encounters with anyone. My life has an impact on my community and my generation has an impact on the generations that follow. Some of that impact is helpful and some of it is really not helpful, and the unhelpful impact leaves a mess behind. Change starts with seeing what is going on and taking responsibility, responsibility starts with the desire and willingness to clean up, and cleaning up starts with an apology.

It will sound strange, but I have only recently learned to start apologising to myself and showing myself kindness. I can see how I bought into the toxic image of masculinity I was sold. I learned to abandon the more vulnerable parts of myself. It was like I said to those parts of me, 'You won't be any use in this demanding world, so I'm going to leave you locked up in a room where no one can see you.' I am now on a new road of befriending myself. In order to do that I catch myself apologising to myself for how I had treated myself and the impact of this self-neglect on how I have been in the world.

Then there is the impact I've had on you. There is so much I could apologise for – the times I was too harsh, or too quick to jump to conclusions, and in particular for the hurt that I caused you with some of the bigger decisions I made with my life. I wrote a long letter to you a few years ago to own up to the ways in which I realise I caused you pain. That apology was necessary to build a stronger relationship for the years that followed.

I also have an impact on my wider relationships and community every day. For example, it's easy to see everything that's wrong in my community as everyone else's fault, but my daily choices make a difference, either positive or negative. If I don't bother to show up to community meetings, talk about others behind their back rather than deal with the issues, or show my anger in places where people were looking for understanding, then I've demonstrated judgement where people needed kindness.

Then there is the impact of my generation on yours. I and we owe you the deepest apology of all for this.

My generation has been the most privileged that has ever existed. I know there are still huge issues of injustice, poverty and violence of every kind. But if you look at it in terms of the history of the world, then my generation has had unprecedented privilege. We are living longer lives that are healthier and wealthier. Child mortality has declined, maternal deaths have gone down, infectious diseases are more easily controlled, vaccinations have increased in number and reach globally, HIV diagnosis rates are declining, and access to healthcare and global communications has improved for so many people.[113]

I witnessed this growing privilege first hand. I remember when the first black-and-white television came to my home, the day we moved into our new mortgaged house from a council-owned house, the arrival of the first fridge and the delivery of an automatic washing machine. Things gradually got better and easier in our household. From the humble beginning of my early childhood we effortlessly became skilled consumers. My parents had good pensions, both ended up having cars, travelled when they chose to and were comfortably off until they died.

So, you may well ask, if things are getting so much better, why apologise? I feel an apology is important because as the most privileged generation that has ever existed, what have we done with it all? Privilege bought us freedom from a lot of hardship, but what we traded was responsibility. We made life easier for ourselves and admittedly for a lot of other people by the accumulation of 'things', thinking they would be the salvation for your future. We ushered in the consumer culture, we thought the great aim of our adult lives was to make life even easier for you than it had been for us and the generations before us. But we forgot something along the way. We wanted to turn our backs on the shameful struggles and hardship of the past, neglecting to examine what made our own parents and grandparents strong, robust and resilient.

When we looked at Mandela and how he became an exceptional elder without considering *how* he became so, we lost sight of, we even despised, the underlying reality of hardship and struggle and its importance in shaping who any of us become.

What have we done with all of our privilege and opportunity? What have we left you with? Economic inequality and climate chaos.

My grandfather had one best set of clothes: one suit and one pair of good shoes. We wanted you to have more, much more. We didn't want you to be sad and disappointed in any way because you couldn't have what you wanted. We didn't want you to be mad with us, so our solution was to indulge you, rather than mentor you. We wanted to secure your love for us and in doing so we robbed you of what you most needed to learn for life – responsibility. Response ability. Being able to respond to what life throws at you. Where do you learn response ability? Through hardship and struggle. It's a fact of life and there are no short cuts. Mandela's defining conclusion on release from twenty-seven years in prison was these words to the watching world: 'With freedom comes responsibility.'[114]

The great change makers of the past century, people like Mandela and Gandhi and Pope John XXIII, can be called alchemists. They managed to dance with the changes of their times and create new solutions for humanity. I'm told that such people have two things in common in their background when they were young – first, they had a near-death experience; and second, they had great responsibility. Struggles and hardships are foundational in our formative years, when we have the potential to strengthen the muscle that will help us develop a purpose, a life's mission, and decide on our values. Ancient wisdom says: 'It is good to bear the yoke (burden) in your youth.'[115] As young people, we need to learn how to figure things out and develop the muscle memory and confidence that remind us we can do it, so that we can creatively solve problems when we become adults. Important studies are now revealing that my generation took away that growth opportunity from you, and you are living with the consequences of our overindulgence and protectiveness. Victor Lipman sums it up well when he asks, 'Has a privileged generation become the screwed generation?'[116]

I remember a memorable conversation with my friend Lennox, about the entitlement he saw in the young people of his home nation, South Africa. 'Mandela had the struggle, but what youth now want is the fruit of the struggle,' he told me. They saw that Mandela had a long walk to freedom, but they didn't realise he was handing on the baton so that they could make their own long walk to freedom. They want the ownership of the land, understandably and rightly, but they don't want the struggle, the hardship, to learn how to work the land and make it profitable. We want jobs with successful companies, but we don't want to work out of our garage sitting on old orange crates in the middle of winter, like their founders did. We want more, but we no longer have any idea how much is enough. We want success now, but we would rather create debt than save. We built all of this privilege, but when we look at the monumental global issues we have left you with, what did we really do with it all?

We all need the grace to embrace humility. To bow a silent knee and say, 'We apologise.'

This need to clean up our act is so fundamental. We must take responsibility, because we cannot assume the moral authority to have eldership-type conversations if we cannot start by cleaning up where we are right now. We need to wake up, be present to ourselves, to our reactions and our actions and their impact, and only then can we move forwards with new choices and better responses.

We need to talk more about this soul-searching subject when we meet next.

Much love

Dad

STARTING A CONVERSATION

1. Discuss the idea of making an apology and talk about what you agree with and disagree with.
2. What does it mean to learn how to struggle in life and what is its value to you? Where are you avoiding struggle and where are you stopping your children from learning to struggle?
3. What areas of your life need an honest conversation in order to move forwards to a better future?

21. Waking up – a call to listen

Hi guys

Nestled in the mountains of Upper Austria, in the Steyr Valley, is an ancient castle, Schloss Klaus. It dates in parts back to the 1400s and the newer parts were built in the 1600s. I still feel deeply privileged that I got to work there under the leadership of Peter Wiegand and Lutz Ketwig. But it was neither of them who caught my attention on the particular morning I'm thinking of. It was a guy called Kurt Schneck, who was being mentored for a senior leadership role at the time. Kurt was speaking boldly to a group of young people from across Europe who had come together for a summer retreat. I can't remember a word he said except for one sentence:

> You are either part of the problem or part of the solution.

That phrase has stuck with me for over forty years.

Maybe it landed on something, a question that had been seeded in me a year earlier, when I was eighteen. You know a group of us were going to travel around Europe as soon as the exams were over, but it ended up being just me, on my own. What I haven't told you was what happened the week before I left England. The Saturday before I set out on was a meltingly hot June day. As a family we had been invited to spend a day with relatives on my mum's side. We had seen them a few times as I was growing up, and each time had seemed quite magical to my young mind because they lived on a working farm in Hertfordshire. They had recently moved to a new house called Langley Lodge, but we had no idea what kind of lodge it was. It was only as we drove up the mile-long farm track and turned left into a dense copse of trees that we emerged into the daylight encircling the house and realised it wasn't a house at all. It was, from my perspective, an impressive mansion with acres of land and its own lake.

That day at Langley Lodge was truly sublime. It felt like I was in a scene from a Merchant Ivory film. The only things missing were the long flowing Edwardian dresses, the riding breeches and being served afternoon tea on the lawn. We actually did dine on the lawn; we wandered the fields, drank fresh lemonade under the trees and attempted croquet in the coarse grass too. But I also remember on this beautiful day having one of those 'time stood still' moments.

I was almost nineteen and had completed the exams that marked the final gateway into that long-awaited adventure we'd been discussing for years called 'the future'. Here I was, on the eve of going off to Europe on my own, but in this silent inner moment it was as if life was giving me a choice. The voice was saying: 'Look at all of this! Surely this is what true success looks like. These people have arrived. Now you have a choice. Do you set out to win the prize of this house – a life focused on you and what you can achieve? Or do you give yourself to the larger issues of a needy world?'

I could viscerally see and feel the choice before me. It would have made a great scene in that film: all the external beauty and grandeur of the day and suddenly, unknown to anyone else, the cameras reveal what is going on inside

Trevor's head. Except this wasn't a film. It actually did happen. I know it sounds like a made-up bit of romantic fancy, but that moment was as real for me as any other in my life.

Would I end up being part of the problem or could I find a pathway to becoming part of the solution?

My experience at Langley Lodge was echoing in my head as Kurt Schneck spoke. I'd had two possible, imagined futures: the Langley Lodge scenario or the alternative, which Jacqueline Novogratz, CEO of Acumen, summed up this way:

> Imagine if we measured success not by the amount of money we earn but instead by the amount of human capacity and flourishing we unleash through our actions. What kind of dream would we allow ourselves?

Let me be clear. There is absolutely nothing wrong with all the splendour of what my relatives owned. I was just challenged by the question: 'What is it all in service of?'

A month after returning from my grand tour of Europe that summer, I got my exam results. I had failed all of them except one and that was a D. It was the most painful event of my life up to that point. The gentle waking whisper of that day at Langley Lodge became a screaming shout on results day: *Wake up!*

This life is not a dress rehearsal. We can't dream or float our way through life, like a leaf carried by a fast-flowing stream. Getting disastrous exam results was the wake-up call of my teenage years, but I've had other wake-ups as I've grown older too. Cancer twice. A charity that, while effective, seemed to live on the edge of grinding to a halt through lack of funding. I was aware too of my dad seeming to fall asleep when he got older. The lights appeared to go out for him sometime in his forties, and by his fifties he had apparently run out of ambition, energy and vision. He chose retirement as early as he could. I can see this dimming of the inner light in my peers too. We all need the challenge to wake up or, more importantly, to stay awake.

On that painful results day I had to wake up to myself. I'd been kidding myself that all was OK, when the results showed it clearly wasn't. What had been going on? I had to wake up to the fact that somewhere within myself I had lost my way. I had to wake up to the fact that emotionally something wasn't right, that I had some growing up to do. I had to wake up to intentionality. I had been unconsciously hoping that a good life would happen by accident. I had to wake up to the fact that I needed to make choices about how I wanted to be in the world and what I would put at the centre of my life – what my life would be in service of. I had to wake up to the fact that living a life of service would involve effort and struggle. I had to wake to the fact that the spiritual path that had engaged me in my mid-teens had become lifeless. All of these faced me as a teenager even before I got my exam results, but I'd been too asleep to realise.

Underneath it all, I had to wake up to the meaning of life itself. Waking up would mean living a conscious life and up to that point I hadn't been. Waking up is about being fully present with who you are, what's going on inside of you, around you and beyond you. Waking up is about allowing yourself to be affected by what is going on in the world and working out your responses to it. Waking up is about being present to the presence of something greater than yourself, or transcendence, or whatever name you give it.

But even deeper than all of this, I had to wake up to learning that there are layers of consciousness (I wish someone had taught me sooner). My Western upbringing attuned me only to the basic levels of owning my thoughts, my decisions and my emotions. I slowly realised that I also needed to wake up to the levels of my unconscious: the 'me' that lives below the waterline, which according to neuroscientists accounts for over 90% of me[117] – what Jung called the shadow side of me, the parts of me that aren't in the light, that I find difficult to be awake to; the thoughts and feelings, the beliefs and motivations, that I didn't want me, let alone others, to see. I began to be awake to seeing that there were even deeper levels of consciousness. Jung called these the collective unconscious, others call them the 'field', the deeper levels of where our individuality is actually joined up to others' existence, others' spirits, a deeper sense of belonging, a deeper sense of 'us' rather than 'me', a deep interconnectedness.

Then I discovered that there is *even more* to wake up to: the possibility and the experience of something transcendent, beyond the natural, hence the name super-natural. Some call it Source, or Divine, or Love, or Ground of all being, or God – whatever. The ultimate depth of life that is the breath within all life. I know I've moved into risky ground for our Western tastes, but my experience of working in India opened my mind and taught me that these levels of waking up are as normal to people there as our rational levels are to us.

Me, you, my friends, your friends have to wake up, otherwise we'll just sleepwalk through life and miss its point, its depth, its opportunity, its meaning. We have to get beyond a Facebook or Instagram life. I didn't say ditch social media, I said we need to wake up and get beyond it.

I was walking out of a little Yorkshire village a few months ago, taking a footpath up into the hills. On the edge of the village the footpath passed a house and I stopped. The garden was immaculate. It was clear that it was the life's work of the owner of the house. Every blade of grass, every inch of flowerbed, was intentionally and perfectly shaped. The gardener's brilliance was evident everywhere. To start with it inspired me, but as I reflected it began to worry me. I wondered if the gardener had time for anything else. Is this what someone should hope for their life when they are seventy? Is this being awake or being obsessive about a self-image of perfection? I don't know the gardener, so who knows the answer to those questions, but it got me thinking.

Last weekend some friends were staying with us and they were telling me about their son buying some new trainers. He wanted Adidas but couldn't afford the real thing, so he bought a replica pair, but even though they were a good imitation, they didn't have the all-important yellow stripes on the back. His peers at school ridiculed him because of the shoes' inadequate branding. The boy was seen as 'less than' because his *shoes* were seen as 'less than'. His self-esteem took a beating from those who were more worried about the presence or absence of a couple of stripes than about the reality of the world that lies ahead of them, a world full of vast challenges.

Waking up is necessary in order to hear the call on our lives. Mandela was awake. He heard the cues, the cries, the spirit of his time. He meditated each day. He searched into every religion to understand the wisdom it held about life's true meaning. He wasn't pursuing success, as it is so often packaged today. Holocaust survivor Viktor Frankl thought the same way:

> Don't aim at success. The more you aim at it and make it a target, the more you are going to miss it.
>
> Success, like happiness, cannot be pursued... it is the unintended side effect of one's personal dedication to a cause greater than oneself, or as the by-product of one's surrender to a person other than oneself.

I have to keep on challenging myself to stay awake and to work out what that looks like with each passing year as I grow older.

With love

Dad

STARTING A CONVERSATION

---

1. Who do you know who seems most awake to themselves – awake to their motives, their consciousness, their life's mission, their values, and their spirit?
2. Take some time to reflect on why you do what you do. Explore what is consciously driving you and possibly what is unconsciously driving you too.
3. What is the most 'awakening' experience you have had that shaped your life? What do you believe about the highest level of meaning for your life?

---

22. Growing up – a call to contain

Hi guys

It's always quite ridiculous to hear an adult shouting 'grow up' to their child. (Did I say that to you? I definitely remember my parents saying it to me, and it was never said as a compliment!) It's funny, because that's exactly what the child is doing – growing up. I'm wondering why parents are so impatient for children to grow up. It's as if we can't wait for you to become adults and then you'll be wise and not make mistakes. There are so many other things a child does that don't get complimented or cheered on, and we end up losing them as we grow up. We lose our natural ability for spontaneity, learning through play, curiosity, spirituality, simplicity, wonder, passion, desire, trust – all these are the gifts of a child. As Christopher Morley says in his poem 'To a Child':

> But there were days, O tender elf,
> When you were Poetry itself!

What does it mean to grow up, and I don't mean just to grow older? Ideally, we would hold on to all those precious gifts I listed and we would add to them wisdom, experience, meaning, courage, generosity and skills. In reality, we unlearn so many good things and we fail to develop the fruits of growth – the wisdom of years, the experience of time, the meaning of life, the courage that comes from hardship and the generosity that comes through loving others.

When we meet a person who doesn't give a hang about anyone else and we see them walk right past someone in great need; when we see a person grandstanding and subtly demanding everyone's attention and praise; when we see a person who is only interested in the wellbeing of their tribe; when we meet a person who has a naïve view on difficult situations; when we meet a person who cannot take feedback and always thinks they are right; when we meet a person who is always talking about themselves and never listening; when we meet a person who acts like everyone and everything exists for them – in each of these instances we see that *they have not grown up.* It is very unattractive and at times, if they find themselves in positions of power or influence, whether at home or work, it is dangerous.

People get older but don't grow up because something within them is damaged or wounded, or something is missing. These deficits happen to many of us when we are young and we spend the rest of our life defending and protecting ourselves against re-experiencing the pain. I've seen you with your own children and I'm certain they know you love them. You can see it by the way they behave around you. You tell them you love them, of course, but also you live love with them. Yet the moment you make that love indulgent, or conditional or inconsistent – one moment love, the next anger, for no apparent reason – then something within them will be hurting, something will be missing. As they grow older this missing piece from their foundational years will begin to skew the shape of their life. They will have to protect what hurts and compensate for what is missing. Hurt and wounded people start to hurt and wound other people. The longer the years go on, the more deeply these defences and compensations become built into the permanent structure of that person's life. Wounded people stay in a state of self-preservation, unaware of others' needs because they use all their energy to protect themselves. In this way, they never grow up. They become a mix of grown-up adult and adapted child, but all within the same adult body, so no one can really make out what is what – until they open their mouth or behave in a childish way. People with emotional damage use a position of power and influence to try to repair the deep damage inside themselves. They look to create a clear pool of influence around them that mirrors back to them a picture their own wonderful self.

We should be thankful that Mandela did the hard personal work of growing up. If he hadn't, his tribal-centric views would have sought black domination over white. He wouldn't have ended Apartheid because he would have been too focused on his own glory to bring together the divided factions. People would have sniffed out his egocentricity early on and not trusted him. He would have become a drain on others, rather than an inspiration. He would have become a divider, not an includer. He would have become a further part of the problem, not a solution. Instead, what he actually said was: 'I don't seek black domination, or white domination, but equality.'

The more public our life becomes, the more our true level of emotional and character development is evident to everyone. We just can't hide it. We can develop all kinds of skills and strategies to get us into positions of power or influence, large or small, but it's only a true level of emotional development that can keep us there without crashing. It's like rugby: one player can leap up high to catch the ball, but only a group of team mates can hold him there. Our emotional development is like that team, providing the muscle within us that keeps us in our position in life. Our gifts and talents can only take us as far as the growth of our character allows. If we're all glitter and no character, our personal house of cards will eventually collapse.

And Mandela continued to do emotional work on himself to ensure that he kept on growing emotionally, not just in his intellect and skills. His commitment to receiving feedback was his way to keep on strengthening his fragile ego. His daily practice of reflection on his character was how he ensured he was growing attributes in his character that helped others, not just glorified himself. To be honest, I think we all need a period of being in therapy as well as developing some truly close friends. We need people who we know love us and who are committed to spotlighting what is lacking in our development. People who can help us see our repeating patterns of behaviour, our over-sensitivities, our subtle hunger for adulation, our safe ways of hiding from others by deferring to them. This is vital. We all carry around within us a little child of some kind - we need to make friends with them and help that part of us to keep on growing, to keep growing up.

It's felt a little strange talking to my own children about growing up, but to be honest it's a necessity that we all never stop developing.

Much love

Dad

STARTING A CONVERSATION

1. What kind of help or input has most helped you to grow up and how?
2. What areas of your life do you see as being less than grown-up and how do you see that affecting the decisions you make or how you treat others?
3. If you had the help of a friendly therapist right now, what area of your life would you want to talk about?

23. Showing up – a call to action

Hi guys

As you know, I spent a good part of my youth cycle racing. We would often get up very early in the morning and cycle out to some A-road to the start of the race, before the traffic got too busy. In those days we could find ourselves cycling to the race in the rain, racing, and then cycling home in the rain. When we got to the start of a race there were rituals to go through: changing into our racing gear, stuffing our normal clothes into a bag and hopefully putting it in someone's car to protect it from the rain. Then there was the warm-up and heading to the start line just in time for the launch into the pain zone that is called cycle racing. We were masochists, to be sure. I always knew that one day I would look back on those times and think that I was completely nuts. Even today when professionals are being interviewed at the end of the race, you can hear conversations like:

Interviewer to cyclist: 'So how did it go?'

Cyclist (shaking their head): 'Nah, didn't go well. I didn't suffer enough.'

When I collapsed off my bike at the end of the race, I would drag myself towards the van serving up hot cups of sweet tea and Mars bars. Next to the tea van and close to the finish line there was usually a massive, two metre square board sitting on an easel. The board had everyone's name, starting position and personal best from previous races, and then the empty box where the officials wrote in your race time for that day's event. This was the moment of heart-fluttering tension. How did I do today and how did my main rivals do? The official would come up to the board, red pen in hand, to write up people's finish times, but occasionally they would single out one of your main rivals and rather than put a time, write the letters D N S. We knew those letters meant only one thing: Did Not Show. They didn't turn up to race. They had all the equipment, the right bike, the right clothes, the right training programme, they even had their name on the start sheet... but they didn't show up and respond to the call to action.

There were other races when a top performer did show up and yet get a very disappointing time, way less than their usual best. You could see the shaking of heads, the looks of bewilderment, and people mumbling as they turned away back to the tea stand: 'What happened?' 'Dunno,' their companion would reply. 'They just didn't show up.'

This time it wasn't that they were absent from the race, they just hadn't brought all of themselves into the race. It isn't just about physically showing up in life, it's *how* we show up that matters.

I guess the simple question I'm asking here is the one I wrote down for myself earlier this morning:

> What will I do with this one life I have, to contribute to the wellbeing of all other lives? How will I show up?

Will I respond to life with a full commitment to action? Will I show up with all my heart, talent and energy?

Maybe I can start by taking a look at how I spend the hours of my day. I can ask myself: '*Who* am I doing this in service of? *What* am I doing this in service of?' These are big questions, I know, but possibly they're the most important ones to answer.

I know that my first reaction to difficult questions is probably to say 'I don't know', but I've learned to say to myself that it's OK *not* to know, because it's only my conscious brain that doesn't know. This is the part of my brain that only holds a maximum of seven bits of information consciously at any one time. So I'm trusting that at some level I probably do know, if I allow myself to sit with the question.

Listening is something I'm having to develop – listening to myself, to what I hear going on around me, to what people are saying, to what I see happening. If I assume I do know, or I don't know, then I hurriedly move on, but keeping the attitude of a learner helps me to sit quietly with a journal or something that can capture my thoughts and jot down what I'm hearing or noticing. I sit patiently with the 'not knowing'.

I listened to a podcast the other day where a woman called Mary was talking about the devastating loss of her twenty-four-year-old son, who had died about a year previously. She was totally bereft, but then I heard her say these words:

> I knew that if I just sat with my grief, just waited, without trying to fix it or make it better, that an invitation would rise up in me, calling me to do something.

Wow! That struck me: 'an invitation would rise up in me, calling me to do something'.

Indeed, an invitation *had* arisen within her and called to her to start a charity that would benefit young people like her son. She showed up.

As well as listening and waiting, I have seen that the easiest thing I can do is simply open my eyes and look around me. What needs doing for the world? Children need someone to read to them, the grass at the local community centre needs cutting, my friend's wheelchair has broken and he can't afford a new one. Don't look for heroes to follow, don't try to become a hero, just show up. Show up and do what you see needs doing with the gifts or talents you have.

That is why Mandela has been such an important mentor to me, and hopefully you, in these conversations, because he didn't set out to be a hero or an elder. Whatever it is that he became, he became it because he just showed up and responded to what life was calling him to be in service of in the world, his specific part of the world at that time. Remember, before anyone knew of him he was sitting in the office of a little Soweto law firm, seeing broken people with desperate problems who needed someone to fight for justice for them in their hidden part of the world. It was work that was out of the public view, it was heart-breaking work, it was poorly paid work, but he was still showing up and dealing with what was in front of him. Mandela had a passion for justice, so he became an unknown lawyer in a local township outside of Johannesburg, and from there he became an unknown activist in that local area. He didn't start with anything other than a heart, a call and a response, doing small things in a (then) unknown community. His influence grew as an outcome, not an aim, of showing up.

I was encouraged recently when I discovered something from Jewish culture. I'd heard of the *bar mitzvah*, the coming-of-age ceremony for a young teenage boy, in which they become a son of the Torah. I hadn't heard of the allied word *mitzvot* (the plural of *mitzvah*), which are simply the little acts you do each day that develop you into a son of the Torah. In English *mitzvot* gets translated as 'commandments', like you're being ordered to do something at the risk of punishment, but actually the word means 'commitments'. What do I want to commit myself to today to make the world a better place? What is the kind word to say, the gracious action, the encouragement, the helping hand, the giving of a little time to support someone? These are the million little things that make up the heart of that core value of loving one another. What discovering this taught me was to focus on showing up in the little things. We know Greta Thunberg as a global activist, but she started out alone, with no support or encouragement, on a little protest of her own about the climate crisis. Such actions are *mitzvot*. They're showing up in the daily little things that life is calling us to, because the danger is that if we focus on the big things then we will never get started.

I'm reminded yet again of those powerful words of Theodore Roosevelt:

> It's not the critic who counts, not the man who points out how the strong man stumbled, or when the doer of deeds could have done better. The credit belongs to the man who is actually in the arena; whose face is marred by dust and sweat and blood; who strives valiantly; who errs and comes short again and again; who knows the great enthusiasms, the great devotions and spends himself in a worthy cause; who at the best, knows in the end the triumph of high achievement; and who at the worst if he fails, at least fails while daring greatly, so that his place

> shall never be with those cold and timid souls who know neither victory or defeat.

The credit belongs to us when we show up, when we get into the mess in front of us, when we answer life's call to serve the needs and issues of our day in some way.

I'm writing to you because you have your life ahead of you and I don't want you to end up in the kind of place where I see so many of my generation have settled. They've set themselves up to retire, draw a pension, play golf, become trivial. I'm not saying there's anything wrong with any of that, but there has to be more to life than that. As I write to you, I'm clearly calling to myself. I am getting older, but am I getting 'elder'? I'm calling to myself to check that I'm responding to the call of life right now, because I see the other subtle call of wanting to linger, to settle, to take it easy. The temptation is there. Do I park my car in a parking lot and leave the engine idling away until it finally runs out of petrol, or do I keep on driving it somewhere meaningful – not heroic, but meaningful? There is a difference.

We might not be able to change the whole world, but we can change the bit of the world around us: the attitudes, the positive or negative 'energy' in conversations, the kind of conversations we have, our investments in people and environment and community. I noticed that when Paul Polman, former CEO of the global company Unilever, retired, he didn't really retire at all. He hasn't sat back; in fact, he's stepped up even more. He ended one chapter and started another. He's set up a foundation and corporation called Imagine to press for the achievement of the UN's Sustainable Development Goals, as well as having a focus on poverty and climate change. Why? Because he's passionate about justice and sustainability. His passion, his call, is bigger than the job he did. It's who he is. And because it's who he is, like Mandela he can keep reinventing what he *does*, to fulfil who he is. We should think of showing up across the whole of our life, more in terms of meaningful chapters and transitioning from one chapter to the next, rather than peaking and lingering.

So here's the call to me, to my generation, to you, to your generation, and to leaders of all ages: Let's show up.

We don't need to be heroes, but if we want to then we should understand what a hero is. Joseph Campbell, the creator of the 'hero's journey', says that a hero is someone who does something in service of something greater than themselves. What are you in service of?

My generation has sadly given you words like 'you are special'. None of us is special, in that we are no more special than anyone else in the world. 'Special' appeals to our ego and is often at the expense of others being 'ordinary'. No one is special and no one is ordinary – we are all *unique*. Each of us has a unique role to play in the world. Special can mean I'm better than you, ordinary can mean I'm less than you, but unique means that I'm equal, but different, to you. We are part of a whole. We are a wave on the ocean, a leaf in the vineyard. We belong to the whole world and we have a unique place in it. I have my role to play and you have yours. I need to respond to the call to find my place in the world and to help you find yours.

One final thought. On mornings when I rush into the day, unconscious of what I'm doing, I often don't spot unhelpful attitudes in myself or notice what's happening around me. It's like I've entered the day with myopia. What I'm coming to terms with is that if I don't show up to myself at the start of the day, show up internally, then it's hard for me to show up for others in the external world. For me personally, showing up internally each morning happens in my meditation and journaling space. It has become my safeguard for how I show up in my actions throughout the day. It's here that I see my impatience, irritation or negative feelings and my optimism, vision or hope – attitudes and emotions that will have a real impact on my day one way or the other. Living a conscious life is about showing up to myself each day.

I'm thinking that maybe I'll put a sign saying 'Show up!' on my desk.

Much love

Dad

STARTING A CONVERSATION

1. What do you see in the world around you right now that makes you say, with some passion, 'That is not OK'?
2. If there was one issue, or one area of need or justice, that you'd like to see change locally, nationally or internationally, what one thing could you do today to take a first step to make a change?
3. How can you ensure that you show up to yourself at the start of each day?

Postscript – an invitation to become an elder

> In a peasant society a person walking with a stout stick, a staff – no longer than an ordinary walking stick and lesser than a pole – is a common sight. One always has it around.
>
> It aids one to maintain a steady, firm gait. It is a crutch one leans on, helps you not to falter in your walk. It is also a weapon to help one defend oneself against any unforeseen danger that may arise in the journey. With it one feels secure and safe.
>
> Such was Xhamela (Walter Sisulu) to me.
>
> —Mandela speaking of the death of Walter Sisulu in 2003

Walter Sisulu was one of Mandela's elders. Sometimes you only really know who your elders are by the loss of them, but Mandela always knew who his were. So did author Mitch Albom.

In 1976, Mitch Albom met Morrie Schwartz. Schwartz was to be one of Albom's professors for the next few years of college. Their first meeting was in Schwartz's office and his invitation to this unknown student was, 'I hope one day we will be friends.' Years later, Albom noticed in a newspaper that Schwartz was seriously unwell. He had enjoyed his classes with Schwartz very much, but despite the commitment to stay in touch, he had never kept that promise. Life had swept him along and he wondered if the old man would even remember him. But once that nagging thought had taken root within him, it wouldn't let him go, and eventually one Tuesday afternoon Albom visited Schwartz.

It was true, Schwartz was very unwell. He was dying of motor neurone disease and probably only had a few more months to live. Albom thought he would be feeling awkward sitting with a dying man he hadn't seen for years, and after some embarrassed conversation he would be out of that house, duty done. Nothing could have been further from the truth. What he thought would be a quick apology and some kindness towards Schwartz turned out to be a complete masterclass in life. In his dying months, Schwartz the older teacher had become Schwartz the elder. He taught Albom about love, living, dying, meaning, purpose, priorities, focus, perspective and hope. An elder doesn't give you a road map on how to live your life now, but rather pours into you the wisdom, the insights, the perspectives that can shape you for a lifetime. Not a map, but a compass. For Albom, that Tuesday with Morrie Schwartz turned into months of Tuesdays with Morrie.[118]

How does anyone become such a person? How do we? We can admire elders like Jimmy Carter, or Graça Machel, or Edith Eger, or even Nelson Mandela, but how do we actually make the journey to becoming our own unique version of Mandela, or Morrie?

I wrote this book because it is not too late to write it. It is not too late for me to be asking myself (and my generation) this question. It is also not too early to be asking my children (and their generation) this question.

I wrote this book as a call to us all. A call to wake up, clean up, grow up and show up.

Most mornings my wife and I do a yoga session, twenty minutes of a whole range of stretches and bends. When we'd finished this morning she turned to me and said, 'What would happen to us if we didn't do this each day?' I replied to the effect that we wouldn't notice it immediately, but every day we do this I feel the effort of having to wake up my muscles, stretch them, keep them fit, make myself uncomfortable for a short time. Yesterday's exercise doesn't get banked for today. If we didn't do this each day, then the tiredness we felt yesterday and again today would just accumulate in our bodies. We would become slower, less flexible, and in time our movements would become limited.

The same is true of life if you don't keep on growing, keep on becoming. It's like particles in a stream that slowly settle and silt up the water bed, reducing its flow and its capacity, eventually making the river itself smaller than it could have been. You are a citizen of the world and you don't need to let the walls of your growing years creep in on you.

Like doing yoga, every day I have the opportunity to begin, to ask myself what I need to do today to become an elder, a Morrie, a Mandela. (I've discovered that wise people start every day as a beginner.) If leadership is anything, it's about keeping our eyes firmly fixed on a desired horizon, fixed like our life depends on it, and then taking one step in that direction. Then another. Then another. In taking each step I have to confront every blockage and obstacle and opportunity that step presents me with, and most of those blocks are inside of me, not outside. Having a purpose behind each step, being intentional, confronting the grief, guilt and self-centredness of my own ego, owning that we can take more steps together than I can do on my own, developing personal depth, wisdom, leadership, courage, resilience, discipline, gravitas and inspiration. Every step is an opportunity to grow the same qualities that we admire in Mandela. Yet Mandela only grew those qualities because of his response to confronting every blockage and obstacle and opportunity that each step of his life posed to him. It was like every step was asking him a question, as it is asking us – 'Who am I becoming?' Mandela answered this question and so can we.

Mitch Albom, as a younger man, almost didn't bother to visit Morrie that first Tuesday and his life would have been impoverished because of it. Many people are in what Jung called the first half of life, where there are jobs to be done, careers to be built, houses to be bought, families to be established, names to be made and identities to be formed. My call to them – to you – is to keep their eyes on the second half of life. It's coming faster than you can imagine. Like starting a pension or savings account in your youth, knowing that you are laying a foundation for your future, those in the first half of life are on a journey to becoming someone. What kind of someone do you want to become? Not an imitation of anyone, but your own original and unique eldership. It's never too late to harvest the wisdom of your years, even in the second half of life. Becoming an elder should be put on young people's radar screens at school and built into organisational leadership development programmes. Who we are becoming should be the personal life agenda for everyone approaching or moving on from midlife. A young person's desire to become an elder will be like a lens to make sense of every obstacle they will surely face in the classroom of life.

Developing as an elder is an intentional journey. It is a necessary struggle to become someone who can contribute meaningfully to this generation and the next. We need to lay out the possibility of such a meaningful life to people from an early age and keep on offering it as the decades accumulate. The importance of the struggle is to break our attachment to our own ego, to free up more and more of that amazing potential that lies within each one of us. Psychology and spirituality have always spoken of this painful but rewarding process as a necessary death, as the only way to discover the new parts of ourselves. Can this be avoided? Sadly not. There are no short cuts to eldership.

German writer and statesman Goethe once said, 'As long as you do not have experience of this dying and becoming, you are only a troubled guest on this earth.' If so, you are not an elder. Speaking of the same process of growth, psychotherapist Frances Weller talked of the tough journey in much the same way when he said, 'This is the hard work of maturation. In the traditional language of apprenticeship, this would be called mastery. In the language of the soul, this is the work of becoming an elder.' He added that the reward is that it makes us 'a source of nourishment for the community... a source of reassurance and stability for the wider community'.[119] This Mandela's 'stout stick, a staff'.

I want to start a conversation. There isn't one area of becoming that we don't all wrestle with. Life is a journey of growth, of transformation, of discovery of meaning and purpose, and it is a journey that we all share – we are all on the same road, even if we're miles apart. In simplistic terms, my children's generation have the energy, the vitality to make things happen, and hopefully those of us in the second half of life have some of the wisdom and perspective of the years. In the Jewish tradition, when groups of people come together for such meaningful conversations they call it a *Bet Midrash* – a House of Learning. That's what I propose for us to create: a conversation, a house of learning, where we help each other to become.

There is a saying in the wisdom literature: 'Wisdom is proved by her children.' Morrie Schwartz shared wisdom with Mitch Albom, elders with youngers, and the proof, the fruit, of the conversations is that our own lives outlive us in the lives of the children (literally or figuratively) that we have invested in.

Let me allow Mandela to have the final words.

> Men and women, all over the world, right down the centuries, come and go. Some leave nothing behind, not even their names. It would seem they never existed at all.[120]

But of the elders who are around today, the ones we are seeking to become, the ones our children will hopefully become one day, his vision, his legacy, was that if they can use

> their collective experience, their moral courage and their ability to rise above the parochial concerns of nation, race and creed, they can help make our planet a more peaceful, healthy and equitable place to live.[121]

What next?

I wrote this book as a starting point for a conversation, a way of getting us going forward and maybe providing some support and accountability along the journey.

In support of your journey, I have created two other free resources:

- *The podcast*: I've developed the podcast *Becoming Mandela* with Dave Courteen. We explore every chapter of the book to enrich your reading experience and to encourage you on your own journey of Becoming (https://anchor.fm/dave-courteen1).
- *The Youth Compass Project*: This is a free online learning experience for young people and for older people who want to know where to start in investing in youth (www.youthcompassproject.com).

Notes

[1] Robin Wall Kimmerer (2020) *Braiding Sweetgrass: Indigenous Wisdom, Scientific Knowledge and the Teachings of Plants*. London: Penguin.
[2] Joseph C. Pearce (2004) *The Biology of Transcendence*. Rochester, VT: Park Street Press.
[3] www.sahistory.org.za/article/african-national-congress-youth-league-ancyl
[4] https://boyanslat.com
[5] www.oneyoungworld.com
[6] https://muhammadyunus.org
[7] www.unfpa.org
[8] Jay Blades (2021) *Making It*. London: Bluebird.
[9] *Life, Interrupted with Simon Thomas*, podcast, 28 June 2021.
[10] Viktor Frankl (2004) *Man's Search for Meaning*. London: Rider Books.
[11] Galatians 6:9, KJV.
[12] Reuel Khoza (2006) *Let Africa Lead*. Johannesburg: Vezubuntu.
[13] Jim Collins (2020) *BE 2.0*. London: Penguin Random House.
[14] Michelle Obama (2018) *Becoming*. London: Viking.
[15] Trevor Waldock (2011) *To Plant a Walnut Tree*. London: Nicholas Brealey Publishing.
[16] Ibid.
[17] www.theelders.org
[18] Arthur Miller (2009) *All My Sons*. Harmondsworth: Penguin.
[19] Rivonia Trial, Pretoria, South Africa, 20 April 1964.
[20] Robben Island, unpublished manuscript, 1975.
[21] 17 December 1998.
[22] Johannesburg, South Africa, 18 July 2008.
[23] Khoza, *Let Africa Lead*.
[24] Dalai Lama & Desmond Tutu (2016) *The Book of Joy*. London: Hutchinson Books.
[25] Letter to Prof. Fatima Meer, 1 March 1971. In Nelson Mandela (2010) *Conversations with Myself*. London: Macmillan.
[26] Richard Stengel (2010) *Mandela's Way: Lessons on Life, Love and Courage*. New York: Crown Publishing Group.
[27] Waldock, *To Plant a Walnut Tree*.
[28] Paul Tournier (1976) *Escape from Loneliness*. London: SCM Press.

[29] From an unpublished manuscript written in prison, in Mandela, *Conversations with Myself.*
[30] Nelson Mandela (1995) *Long Walk to Freedom*. London: Abacus.
[31] www.theoceancleanup.com
[32] Pearce, *The Biology of Transcendence.*
[33] Plenary talk, One Young World conference, October 2019.
[34] 'County lines' is running drugs between counties and from towns into rural areas using young people, in order to protect the drug bosses.
[35] Presidential Inaugural Speech, 10 May 1994, Pretoria, South Africa.
[36] Rivonia Trial, Pretoria, South Africa, 20 April 1964.
[37] https://twitter.com/fmlappe/status/774722741043884032.
[38] www.bigissue.com
[39] www.bbc.co.uk/programmes/p06y23y9
[40] https://bailproject.org/team/robin-steinberg
[41] Bill Hybels (2007) *Holy Discontent: Fuelling the Fire That Ignites Personal Vision.* Grand Rapids, MI: Zondervan.
[42] Joseph Campbell (1990) *The Hero's Journey*. New York: HarperCollins.
[43] Dawna Markova (2000) *I Will Not Die an Unlived Life: Reclaiming Purpose and Passion*. Newbury Port, MA: Conari Press.
[44] Mountaineer W.H. Murray (1951) *The Scottish Himalayan Expedition*. London: J.M. Dent.
[45] http://edition.cnn.com/2008/WORLD/africa/06/24/mandela.quotes/
[46] Markova, *I Will Not Die an Unlived Life.*
[47] Rivonia Trial, Pretoria, South Africa, 20 April 1964.
[48] Richard Reed (2018) *If I Could Tell You One Thing*. Edinburgh: Canongate Books.
[49] www.charitywater.org
[50] www.mercyships.org.uk
[51] From an unpublished autobiographical manuscript written on Robben Island in 1975. In Nelson Mandela (2013) *Nelson Mandela by Himself*. London: Macmillan.
[52] www.alcoholics-anonymous.org.uk
[53] Samantha Power (US Ambassador to the UN 2013–17) (2019) *The Education of an Idealist*. London: William Collins.
[54] Speech at London School of Economics, 6 April 2000.
[55]
www.ted.com/talks/majd_mashharawi_how_i_m_making_bricks_out_of_ashes _and_rubble_in_gaza
[56] Reed, *If I Could Tell You Just One Thing.*

[57] Nahum Ward-Lev (2019) *The Liberating Path of the Hebrew Prophets.* Maryknoll, NY: Orbis Books.
[58] Kevin and Jackie Freiberg (2018) Madiba leadership: 5 lessons Nelson Mandela taught the world about change. *Forbes*, 19 July. https://www.forbes.com/sites/kevinandjackiefreiberg/2018/07/19/madiba-leadership-5-lessons-nelson-mandela-taught-the-world-about-change/?sh=3af5ebc641ba
[59] Mandela, *Nelson Mandela by Himself.*
[60] Interview with Charles Villa-Vicencio, Johannesburg, 1993. In ibid.
[61] Robben Island, 1 February 1975.
[62] Ken Wilber (2017) *A Brief History of Everything*. Boulder, CO: Shambhala; (2007) *Up from Eden*. Wheaton, IL: Quest Books; (2017) *The Religion of Tomorrow*. Boulder, CO: Shambhala.
[63] https://integrallife.com/wake-grow-edge-unknown-human-being
[64] www.myersbriggs.org
[65] Address to Parliament of the World's Religions, Cape Town, South Africa, December 1999.
[66] Abraham Joshua Heschel (2013) *I Asked for Wonder* (ed. Samuel Dresner). Chestnut Ridge, NY: Crossroad Publishing.
[67] Richard Stengel (2012) *Nelson Mandela: Portrait of an Extraordinary Man.* London: Virgin Digital.
[68] Mandela, *Long Walk to Freedom.*
[69] Stengel, *Nelson Mandela.*
[70] Excerpt from the speech 'Citizenship in a Republic', delivered at the Sorbonne in Paris, France on 23 April 1910.
[71] Allister Sparks (2013) 'Nelson Mandela: A world statesman who made time for everyone', *Guardian*, 7 December 2013.
[72] Mandela, *Conversations with Myself.*
[73] T.S. Eliot (2001) *The Four Quartets*. London: Faber & Faber.
[74] Luke 7:35, NIV.
[75] https://theconversation.com/what-archbishop-tutus-ubuntu-credo-teaches-the-world-about-justice-and-harmony-84730
[76] Stengel, *Nelson Mandela.*
[77] Nelson Mandela Foundation video, 2006.
[78] Mandela, *Long Walk to Freedom.*
[79] On receiving the Chris Hani Award, Johannesburg, 1 July 1998.
[80] Dalai Lama & Tutu, *The Book of Joy.*
[81] Johan Pottier (2009) *Re-Imagining Rwanda: Conflict, Survival and Disinformation in the Late Twentieth Century*. Cambridge: Cambridge University Press.

[82] John O'Donohue (2008) 'For a Leader', in *To Bless the Space Between Us*. New York: Convergent Books.
[83] Stengel, *Mandela's Way*.
[84] https://hellemanworld.blogspot.com/2013/12/nelson-mandela-1918-2013-some-personal.html
[85] Nassim Taleb (2013) *Antifragile*. Harmondsworth: Penguin.
[86] Ken Wilber (2001) *Grace and Grit*. Boulder, CO: Shambhala.
[87] Mandela, *Long Walk to Freedom*.
[88] Victoria Derbyshire (2019) 'Victoria Derbyshire on life after breast cancer – and baring all on television. *The Times Magazine*, 4 May.
[89] www.forbes.com/2006/09/22/trust-economy-markets-tech_cx_th_06trust_0925harford.html#3226f8212e13
[90] Mandela, *Long Walk to Freedom*.
[91] Full transcript: http://db.nelsonmandela.org/speeches/pub_view.asp?pg=item&ItemID=NMS010&txtstr=prepared%20to%20die
[92] www.oneyoungworld.com
[93] Howard Gardner (1997) *Leading Minds*. London: Harper Collins.
[94] Presidential address to ANC Youth League Conference, December 1951.
[95] Mandela, *Long Walk to Freedom*.
[96] Peter Hawkins & Nick Smith (2007) *Coaching, Mentoring and Organizational Consultancy*. Maidenhead: Open University Press.
[97] Nelson Mandela & Mandla Langa (2017) *Dare Not Linger: The Presidential Years*. London: Macmillan.
[98] Mandela, *Long Walk to Freedom*.
[99] Hebrews 12.11.
[100] *Newsweek*, 7 August 1990.
[101] Letter to Makgatho Mandela, Robben Island, 28 July 1969.
[102] 13 April 1990.
[103] *Newsweek*, 7 August 1990.
[104] Makoto Fujimura (2020) *Art and Faith*. New Haven, CT: Yale University Press.
[105] From a conversation with Richard Stengel, 9 March 1993.
[106] www.justice.gov.za/trc
[107] Desmond Tutu (2000) *No Future without Forgiveness*. London: Rider Books.
[108] Khoza, *Let Africa Lead*.
[109] Mandela, *Conversations with Myself*.
[110] Charlie Mackesy (2019) *The Boy, the Mole, the Fox and the Horse*. London: Ebury Press.

[111] Mandela, *Long Walk to Freedom.*
[112] Lincoln University, 6 June 1961.
[113] For data see Victor Lipman (2012) Has a privileged generation become the screwed generation? *Forbes*, 26 July. https://www.forbes.com/sites/victorlipman/2012/07/26/has-a-privileged-generation-become-the-screwed-generation/#26aa4c0a2309; and Hans Rosling & Osla Rosling (2019) *Factfulness*. London: Sceptre.
[114] Mandela, *Long Walk to Freedom.*
[115] Lamentations 3:27.
[116] Lipman, Has a privileged generation become the screwed generation?
[117] Iain McGilchrist (2009) *The Master and His Emissary: The Divided Brain and the Making of the Western World. New Haven.* CT: Yale University Press.
[118] Mitch Albom (2003) *Tuesdays with Morrie*. London: Sphere.
[119] Francis Weller (2015) *The Wild Edge of Sorrow*. Berkeley, CA: North Atlantic Books.
[120] From an unpublished sequel to his autobiography written in 1998, published in Mandela, *Nelson Mandela by Himself.*
[121] Johannesburg, South Africa, 18 July 2008.

Acknowledgements

To all the hidden elders across my life: Eddie, Nahum, Gilly, Marion, Lutz, Peter, Ron, Lakshmi and Brendan.

I've never had a writing coach before, but Jacqui Lofthouse went way more than the extra mile in her encouragement, her integrity, her honesty and care.

To Peter Hawkins, because he was a generous elder to me in this book as with *To Plant a Walnut Tree*. He challenged me, disrupted my thinking, turned my ideas inside out, but most of all believed that this is a book that needed to be written.

To the early readers of this book, Ralph Holtom, Louise Ronnerdahl and Dave Courteen, who not only read the book but were so enthusiastic about creating a podcast to go with it. Thank you for investing your time and encouragement.

To Andy Steward, whose encouragement, generosity of time and spirit made the book look good.

To my journey-fellows Jane, Paul, Georg, Liz, Michael, Louise and Julian.

To the wonderful team I was part of at Emerging Leaders.

To Sally Osborn, once again, for her editorial excellence.

But above all to Jane, who has walked with me through this process with a ferocious love that has constantly challenged me to get over myself, so that I could find my better self and undoubtedly write a better book.

Printed in Great Britain
by Amazon

69133590R00142